Private Healthcare in the OECD: A Canadian Perspective

PHILIPPE CYRENNE
(with MARIAN SHANAHAN)

Copyright © 2002 University of Toronto

All rights reserved. No part of this publication may be reproduced, stored in a retrieval system, or transmitted in any form or by any means, electronic, mechanical, photocopying, recording, or otherwise, without the prior written permission of the publisher.

Canadian Cataloguing in Publication Data

Library and Archives Canada Cataloguing in Publication

Cyrenne, Philippe, 1956-
    Private healthcare in the OECD : a Canadian perspective /
Philippe Cyrenne ; with Marian Shanahan.

(Monograph series on public policy and public administration ; 13)
Includes bibliographical references.
ISBN 0-7727-8615-1

1. Medical care—OECD countries. 2. Medical care—OECD countries—
    Finance. 3. Medical care—Canada. 4. Medical care—Canada—Finance.
5. Medical policy—OECD countries. 6. Medical policy—Canada.
    I. Shanahan, Marian II. University of Toronto. Centre for Public
    Management III. Title. IV. Series.

RA413.C97 2004   362.1   C2004-905577-1

Printed for the University of Toronto Centre for Public Management by University of Toronto Press.

TABLE OF CONTENTS

PREFACE   vii

I INTRODUCTION   1

    1.1 Summary   1

    1.2 Introduction   2

II HEALTHCARE SYSTEMS – THE MARKET FOR PRIVATE GOODS AND THE MARKET FOR HEALTHCARE SERVICES   4

    2.1 The Market for Private Goods   4

    2.2 The Market for Healthcare Services   6

III HEALTHCARE SYSTEMS – A CONCEPTUAL OVERVIEW   10

    3.1 Types of Healthcare Systems   10

    3.2 Public Healthcare Systems: Funding Approaches   10

    3.3 Coverage   12

    3.4 Administration   14

    3.5 Definitions of Private and Public Healthcare   14

IV AN OVERVIEW OF THE HEALTHCARE SYSTEMS OF SELECTED OECD COUNTRIES   16

    4.1 The UK Healthcare System   16

4.2 The French Healthcare System	26
4.3 The German Healthcare System	33
4.4 The Belgian Healthcare System	39
4.5 The Swedish Healthcare System	46
4.6 The Australian Health System*	53
4.7 Views of the Market Oriented Reforms in the OECD	61
4.8 Summary of the Selected Healthcare Systems	64
V ISSUES IN THE OPERATION AND PERFORMANCE OF HEALTHCARE SYSTEMS	**67**
5.1 Issues Related to the Allocation System	67
5.2 Issues Related to Health Insurance	75
5.3 Issues Related to Competition between Healthcare Providers	81
5.4 Issues Related to the Total Funding of the System	86
VI ISSUES IN THE REGULATION OF A PRIVATE HEALTHCARE SECTOR	**92**
6.1 Competition at the Insurance Stage	92
6.2 Competition at the Provider Stage	95
6.3 General Regulatory Issues to be Addressed	97
VII MODELS OF PARALLEL PUBLIC AND PRIVATE HEALTHCARE SYSTEMS	**102**

---

* Written by Marian Shanahan

7.1 Competition between Firms Providing Different Varieties   103

7.2 Competition between Firms Providing Different Qualities   104

7.3 Discussion   107

7.4 Empirical Evidence – For Profit versus Not for Profit Hospital Care   108

VIII CONCLUSION   109

REFERENCES   111

ENDNOTES   122

Private Healthcare in the OECD: A Canadian Perspective

Philippe Cyrenne**
Professor, Department of Economics
The University of Winnipeg

December 12, 2003
(Revised)

* This project was funded through a grant from the Donner Foundation. Additional funds were received from the University of Winnipeg Major Research Program. I would like to thank Tara Kuzyk and Anna Birtles for their able research assistance. I would also like to thank the numerous healthcare officials in the respective OECD countries for a number of helpful discussions. Helpful comments were received from two anonymous referees as well as the Editor of the Monograph series, Andrew Stark. I am responsible for any errors or omissions.

** The section on the Australian healthcare system was written by Marian Shanahan, Health Economist, National Drug and Alcohol Research Centre, University of New South Wales Sydney, NSW, 2052, Australia.

PREFACE

In *Private Health Care in the OECD*, Philippe Cyrenne provides the first comprehensive look at the health-care systems of other major democracies from a Canadian perspective. Specifically, *Private Health Care* focuses on the UK, France, Germany, Belgium, Sweden and (in a chapter contributed by Marian Shanahan) Australia.

In contrast to the United States, all of these countries share a commitment to universal coverage. By contrast with Canada, they have embarked further down the road toward integrating private-sector involvement in health-care delivery and financing.

Much of what's intriguing about Cyrenne's discussion lies in the details of his individual country-by-country analyses. But some broad themes emerge. When it comes to health-care delivery—in other words, when the question is the extent to which health care should be publicly or privately *supplied*—current Canadian debate centers around the issue of whether hospitals should be privatized in the way that physician services already have been. Notably, all the OECD countries under analysis have taken that step to some degree, and Cyrenne offers a case-by-case discussion of how successfully such innovations have coalesced with the principle of universal care.

When it comes to health-care financing—in other words, when the question is the extent to which health care should be publicly or privately paid for—three observations emerge from Cyrenne's analysis. First, unlike Canada, in which basic physician services are free for everyone, all the OECD countries under analysis require some form of co-payment from those above a certain income level. Second, unlike Canada, where basic hospital services are free, all the OECD countries under analysis with the exception of Australia require, again, some kind of co-payment from those who can afford it. Finally, like Canada, none of the countries under analysis—with the partial exception of Australia—has gone the way of the United States in instituting any widespread form of managed care, in which physicians are given a financial incentive *not* to treat patients.

What this suggests is that if a system is going to impose incentives against unnecessary treatment, it's better that the patient face them in the form of co-payments than that the physician face them in the form of managed care. There is a basic intuition at work here. As a patient, I would rather that it be me who has to wrestle with the incentive not to seek treatment than worry that my doctor has an incentive not to offer it. Co-payments are more consistent with patient control.

But co-payments are only part of the repertoire of private payment; more important is the possibility of private insurance coverage that allows private access to services that would otherwise remain available under the public system: in other words, two-tier medicine. Many of the countries under analysis have taken explicit steps in this direction, while Canada has not. The acid test, politically, is whether such access improves the waiting times while preserving the quality of service in the public system. Here, the record is mixed and the devil is in the details: you have to read Cyrenne's lucid analysis for yourself.

All in all, Cyrenne shows, France, Germany and Belgium have managed to provide universal coverage with significant patient choice and a limited amount of direct government involvement in the day-to-day management of the system. Australia, Sweden, the U.K. and Canada, by contrast, have not. The difference, as Cyrenne argues, lies in the degree to which the various systems have become "politicized."

Private Health Care in the OECD is the thirteenth monograph in the University of Toronto Centre for Public Management Monograph Series, which is funded by a generous grant from the Donner Canadian Foundation.

Andrew Stark
Editor

CHAPTER I

INTRODUCTION

1.1 SUMMARY

In all OECD countries, the performance and future viability of the healthcare system is an ongoing topic of discussion. This is particularly true for the countries analyzed in this study, United Kingdom, France, Germany, Belgium, Sweden and Australia. These countries were selected for the study for a number of reasons. The British, French, German and Belgian systems were chosen based on their longevity and the central role that universal, or near-universal, coverage plays. Sweden, long identified with the welfare state, is a good example of a system evolving under the fiscal strains related to rising healthcare costs. Australia is a useful model for Canada, given its British heritage, its federal system, and its low population density.

A number of common threads can be discerned. First, there is the ongoing trade off between accessibility and cost control. Liberal policies of patient choice and health service provision are at odds with a desire for global cost containment. Second, there is the ongoing discussion of how to introduce greater efficiencies into the system. This ranges from an increase in control over the health system through planning to an emphasis on market-like features, such as public-private sector contracts including private hospitals. Third, there is a remarkable variation in the use of the private sector, which has a significant role in all the healthcare systems in this study. For example, in the UK, despite a renewed emphasis on the public healthcare system, involving an increase in 50% in cash terms for the public system, the private sector is seen as too important to abandon. Apart from financing the construction of new hospitals, the private sector is also seen as a partner in which public health services can be provided in private hospitals. In France, supplementary insurance is extensive and is supported by the government as a way of reducing the tax burdens of employers and employees. Payroll costs to employees and employers are a useful signal of the ups and downs of healthcare costs. In addition, the French healthcare system requires payments be made to physicians, with most of the cost reimbursed through a combination of public and private insurance.

A number of conclusions emerge from the analysis in this study. First, all countries are grappling with the issues of patient choice and cost containment. In addressing these twin issues, a variety of approaches have been taken and a number of experiments in delivery are being considered. Second, all countries maintain a commitment to universal healthcare coverage, which leads to a considerable degree of redistribution. Third, in countries with an insurance-based system, there is a heightened tension between third party public insurers and the government. Governments consider cost control important for competitive reasons, which brings them into conflict with arms' length public insurers who must satisfy the increasing demands and expectations of patients and providers. Fourth, a key question appears to be the following: how can efficiencies be enhanced in the healthcare system while at the same time maintaining the elements of redistribution in the system? The countries examined in this study address this issue in different ways, with the particular policies chosen influenced by their respective approaches to social policy.

1.2 INTRODUCTION

A number of OECD countries are wrestling with issues and problems related to their healthcare systems. Common to all of them is the challenge of marrying the goal of universal healthcare access with a desire to control the claims made on the public purse. Different countries have pursued this common objective via a variety of methods, despite the similarity of their objectives.

This study is designed to focus on a particular issue that has arisen in a number of these countries, specifically, the role of the private sector in the delivery of healthcare. In addressing this issue, this study examines a number of countries which have a predominantly public healthcare system: the UK, France, Germany, Belgium, Sweden and Australia. This study will also look at a number of recent proposals to reform those systems.

While the research is particularly directed to the role of the private sector, it will be necessary to provide a brief overview of the healthcare systems in each country. Although there have been several recent analyses of the respective healthcare systems, the focus in this study will be on a number of regulatory issues that arise in any discussion of a possible increased role for the private sector as well on recent reform trends and issues.[1]

Apart from a summary of the present state of the above mentioned healthcare systems, a major goal of the study will be to place these systems and proposed changes in context. I will do this by relating the role of the private sector in healthcare with the role of the private sector more generally in providing similar goods and services. While many of the points raised are familiar to healthcare economists, a goal will be to highlight this issue for the nonspecialist.

All studies have their strengths and limitations. The goal of this study is to examine the healthcare systems from a regulatory point of view, which is central to the issue of the coexistence of a public and private sector healthcare sector. In doing so, I highlight a number of important economic issues that arise when this dual system exists. Much current research in health economics focuses on empirical studies related to the efficacy of a dual public and private system. Although these issues will be briefly discussed, the sheer volume of material would expand the study beyond manageable limits, and shift the focus from the regulatory issues raised here.

CHAPTER II

HEALTHCARE SYSTEMS – THE MARKET FOR PRIVATE GOODS AND THE MARKET FOR HEALTHCARE SERVICES

Prior to a discussion of the healthcare systems analyzed in this study, it will be helpful to first outline the differences between the market for healthcare and markets for similar goods and services. As will be seen the source of much of the debate regarding the appropriate role for government in the financing and delivery of healthcare can be traced to this issue.

2.1 THE MARKET FOR PRIVATE GOODS

For ordinary market-provided goods, consumers purchase the respective goods or services from a number of privately-owned firms. Firms hire labour, capital and other inputs to provide the service with the objective of profit maximization. Assuming that the firms do not agree to fix outputs or prices, their supply decisions will result in an overall industry supply of the good. Firms post prices for the good, whose characteristics are known to the consumer. If the market is competitive, firms compete for the consumer's dollar by providing the good or service at the lowest possible price (an output consistent with marginal cost).

Given market demand aggregated over consumers and the supply decisions of firms, the competitive outcome yields a price and a total quantity demanded and supplied of the service. Depending on the cost conditions underlying the production of the good or service, there may be a number of firms existing in equilibrium. If the market demand is sufficient, and the cost conditions are such that the individual firms have U-shaped average cost curves, then the long run competitive equilibrium is an outcome where the price of the service equals long run marginal cost and all firms in the industry earn normal profits. This market outcome scores the highest in terms of the common efficiency standard used by economists.[2]

For some type of goods, in particular, goods for which there is infrequent and unexpected demand, consumers purchase insurance in order

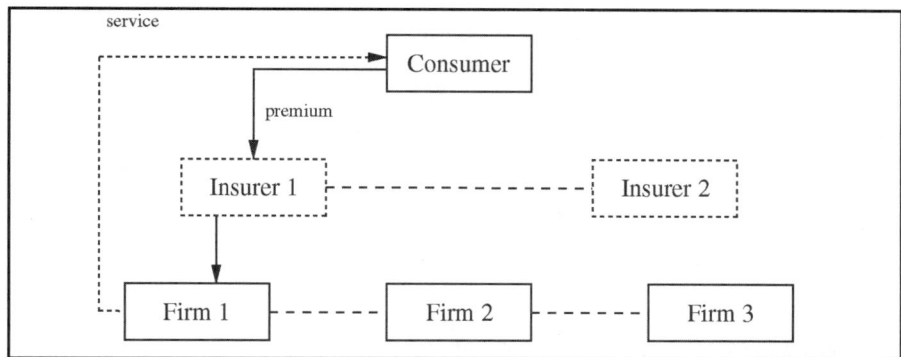

Figure 1: The Market for Private Goods

to cover the costs of the service. Figure 1 depicts the relationship between consumers and firms and as well as a set of insurers, who are used by consumers to reduce the risks of large unexpected costs, for example, dental insurance, car insurance, and home insurance. In return for a premium paid to an insurer, the consumer is entitled to service from firms whose costs are covered by the insurer. Also indicated in Figure 1 are dotted lines between insurers and firms which indicate the possibility of competition between firms at those levels.

By pooling risks which are not perfectly correlated, the insurer can provide coverage (or compensation) for the loss in exchange for a premium paid to the insurer. It must be mentioned that once a claim is made with the insurer, the legitimacy of the claim must be verified by an insurance adjuster who first decides whether the accident is covered by the contract, and then approves the payment for the repairs. In most cases, the insurer provides the duties of the insurance adjuster as part of the insurance contract. In other words, the insurance function and the insurance adjuster duties are often integrated within a single firm. The premium charged to a consumer is related to the risk brought into the pool by the individual, with riskier individuals asked to pay a higher premium, if they can be identified by the insurer.[3] If the insurance market is competitive, indicated by the horizontal line between insurers, all insurers make normal profits, which occurs when the total premiums received equal the total payouts plus the cost of administering the insurance plan.[4]

For private insurance coverage, the higher the cost of an accident and/or the higher the probability of an accident, the higher the premium that must be charged. In cases when there is no benefit from risk pooling, and the probability of an accident is equal to one, then the premium just equals the cost of the accident. This is equivalent to paying for costs out of pocket. In some cases, where the probability of a claim being made is relatively high, insurance companies put an upper limit on the total payouts that can be made to an insured person. For example, orthodontic care for children often has a total dollar limit of coverage specified in the parent or guardian's dental insurance contract.

2.2 THE MARKET FOR HEALTHCARE SERVICES

As with other risks where the cost in the event of a bad outcome or accident is large, medical insurance has been used to reduce the welfare losses from illness or accident. Given the likelihood that healthcare services will be required at some point in a person's life, risk aversion on the part of consumers leads to the demand that these costs be paid through insurance. That is, the possibility of enormous costs, and the necessity of treatment, make insurance coverage both desirable and necessary.[5] The benefits to risk pooling make insurance purchase more efficient than out of pocket payment for healthcare.[6]

Note, however, given that the premiums are set prior to the occurrence of illness, the insurer and the consumer must agree on the particular illnesses or accidents that will be covered and hence on the treatment required. In Figure 2, we have an insurer who, in exchange for premiums paid, will cover the costs of medical treatment if required. The figure indicates a slightly more complex setting than is illustrated in Figure 1. Figure 2 indicates the consumer must go through the insurer, who checks to see whether the particular claim is covered by the contract, and if so, then approves the subsequent services provided by the General Practitioner, Specialist, and Hospital.[7]

The solid lines going from the Insurer represent payments for services provided by the General Practitioner, Specialist and Hospital. The dotted lines represent the services provided to the patient. For medical insurance, there is also an information flow between the GP/Hospital/Specialist and Insurer in order to verify that the medical treatment is covered by the insurance contract.

It is important to note that the insurer could be private or public. In Figure 2, two separate insurers are listed, which would be replaced by a

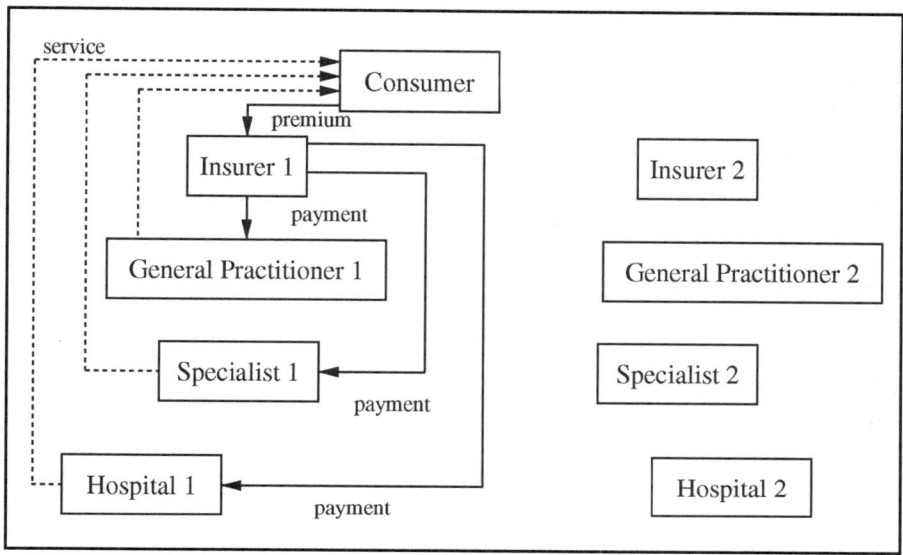

Figure 2: The Market for Healthcare Services

single insurer in the case of a single public insurer or a private firm with a monopoly over health insurance. Insurer 1 and 2 maybe private for-profit firms or private not-for-profit third parties, such as sickness funds in Germany and Belgium.

In a full information world, should an accident or illness occur, consumers would be aware of the particular treatment required and would seek treatment depending on the coverage specified in the insurance contract. The quality of service that can be chosen by the consumer depends on the nature of the insurance coverage, but for a given quality of service the insurer would prefer that the consumer choose the firm (hospital) offering the lowest price. Profit-maximizing firms (hospitals) would compete for the patronage of the consumer, and assuming no local monopoly power, sufficient market demand, and U-shaped average costs, the services would be provided at the efficient level where price equals long-run marginal cost and hospitals earn zero economic profits.

Many observers of the healthcare system argue that the full-information assumption is inappropriate for the healthcare market. Other goods for which the full information assumption can be questioned are repairs to computers, or repairs to automobiles. It has been argued that consumers experiencing symptoms do not know what treatment, if any, is required. In this case, the consumer must acquire information regarding the nature of medical intervention if any that is needed. In Figure 2, this puts a second stage between consumers and firms (hospitals). In the healthcare literature, this is referred to as the Gatekeeper role, often filled by the General Practitioner (GP). An important task of the GP is to reduce the uncertainty regarding the reason for the symptoms, and once identified, provide treatment. However, if additional uncertainty exists or treatment requires specialized medical treatment, the consumer is referred to a specialist.

There is some debate about whether there are sufficient incentives in the hospital system to ensure that only the medically necessary treatment is delivered. Ensuring that only medically-necessary services are delivered falls under the General Practitioners' Gatekeeper responsibilities. Also shown in the diagram is the possibility that consumers may have direct access to a specialist, which has been the practice in a number of countries studied here, for example Germany. Some healthcare economists feel a fee-for-service compensation scheme for general practitioners and specialists leads to the provision of an excessive level of medical services.

An important issue related to Figure 2 is the way in which the various components of the healthcare system can be structured. Each component, the insurer, the general practitioner, specialist and hospital can be an independent autonomous unit. In contrast, for many other private goods provided by insurance, the delivery of the service is undertaken to some extent by integrated firms. For example, the insurer may employ insurance adjusters (who play a Gatekeeper role). In the healthcare system, it is clear that some, if not all, of the stages – insurer, GP, specialist and hospital – could be integrated under common ownership. For example, at one extreme, an insurer could employ general practitioners and specialists and own and operate a hospital in a completely vertically integrated system. In between are various degrees of integration; for example, an insurer may own a hospital and contract with independent general practitioners and/or specialists. Or a group of specialists may own a clinic or hospital.

On the surface it appears that the additional stages of information acquisition and insurance purchase make healthcare markets quite similar to certain other private services, such as dental care or automobile repair. These two industries provide the services privately, and have a substantial fraction of the costs covered by insurance. However, there are a number of additional differences in how the public healthcare systems operate in the countries analyzed here which gives rise to the variety of healthcare systems in existence.

In the next section, I provide an overview of the healthcare systems analyzed in this study. As will be seen, there is a remarkable variety in the role played by the private sector in this countries.

CHAPTER III

HEALTHCARE SYSTEMS – A CONCEPTUAL OVERVIEW

3.1 TYPES OF HEALTHCARE SYSTEMS

It is possible to classify the healthcare systems in this study into two broad categories: Social Insurance-based systems, as in Germany, France, Belgium; and Social Security or Social Welfare-based systems, as in the UK, Sweden, Australia or Canada. The distinction is that in the former the healthcare system is based on insurance principles, in that citizens pay explicit premiums which entitle them to explicit benefits. This requires the existence of an insurer, which might be a nonprofit organization, a public corporation, or in some cases a for-profit insurance company. In Social Welfare-based systems, discussions of the link between taxes paid and benefits received are not framed in terms of either an explicit or implicit insurance contract, but are discussed along the lines of social security.[8] That is, individuals are entitled to care as a condition of citizenship, as a right to which they are entitled, independent of contribution. This is much like social assistance for low-income individuals.

3.2 PUBLIC HEALTHCARE SYSTEMS: FUNDING APPROACHES

In terms of financing public healthcare systems, two general approaches are used: financing healthcare costs out of general revenues, as in the UK, Sweden, Australia and Canada, or financing based primarily on employment, as in Germany, Belgium, France. The former is chosen by Social Welfare-based systems, while the latter is a characteristic of Social Insurance-based systems. In Social Welfare-based systems, the general revenues may come from income, personal and corporate, sales or value-added taxes. There is no attempt to link the taxes paid to any particular type of healthcare coverage.

In Social Insurance-based systems, the funding of the healthcare system is based largely on employment, income or payroll taxes. For example, in Germany, all employed individuals and their employees pay healthcare premiums which are related to their employment income.[9] This is similar to the Employment Insurance program in Canada where employers and employees contribute to a fund which compensates eligible individuals who are unemployed. In Social Insurance-based systems, provision must be and is made for individuals who are unemployed, with the premiums paid by the state. Otherwise, benefits are provided in kind, as in a Social Welfare-based system.

It is also possible for there to be additional charges for services, which come in the form of co-payments or coinsurance, which exists in Social Insurance-based systems like Belgium, France and Germany. This is consistent with the insurance-based nature of these systems. For example, insurance contracts for automobile insurance generally include deductibles, which is that part of the loss that is not covered by the insurer. Specifically, individuals may be asked to pay a portion of the bill for health services as in Belgium. Such co-payments – often termed user fees – can also be used as a supplementary form of financing as in the Social welfare-based systems of Australia, Sweden and the UK. In these cases, additional revenues are based on healthcare usage.

It is likewise possible for healthcare premiums to be used as a supplementary form of income for Social Welfare-based systems, as with the healthcare premiums levied by the Canadian provinces Alberta and British Columbia. For example, in Canada, the provinces of British Columbia and Alberta levy healthcare premiums which go to support the publicly-funded system, topping up the funding coming out of general revenues. For example, in British Columbia premiums are based on family size and income, with the following monthly rates: $54 for one person, $96 for a family of two, and $108 for a family of three or more.[10] The premiums must be paid one month in advance, and beneficiaries may pay directly to the Medical Services Plan, or through payroll or pension deduction. The British Columbia plan offers assistance with the payment of premiums to Canadian citizens or landed immigrants, ranging from 20 to 100 percent, and based on an individual's net income for the two preceding tax years (subject to deductions for age, family size and disability). The Alberta plan operates in a similar manner, with two regular premium rates: one for individuals with no dependants ($44 per month) and one for families ($88 per month).[11] Payment may be made through direct deduction from the beneficiary bank account, with low income and senior citizens qualifying for premium subsidies.

An important trend is for Social Insurance-based systems to receive additional monies in the form of general grants from governments in order to supplement the revenues taken in through payroll taxes, the primary source of revenue for the Social Insurer.

3.3 COVERAGE

(a) Mandatory versus Voluntary

A third major way in which healthcare systems can differ has to do with whether participation in a health plan is mandatory or voluntary. Participation is mandatory in the Social Insurance-based systems analyzed here. For example, the German healthcare system requires that all citizens join a "sickness" fund. This is in contrast to voluntary systems, such as the United States, where consumers have the option of not purchasing health insurance. The mandatory feature in Social Insurance-based systems is made operational by employment. For example, in the German system, contributions are required from all employees and employers. In Social Insurance-based systems, healthcare coverage of the unemployed is much like the coverage for individuals in Social Welfare-based systems.

The percentage of the population covered for health costs varies little in the set of countries examined here (see Table 1). For comparison purposes, the US voluntary system results in 45% of the population being covered for 2001. However, more variation exists in pharmaceutical coverage, with a low of 12% for the US and 50% for Canada to 100% coverage in Australia, Sweden and the UK for 2004.[12]

(b) Comprehensive versus Limited

Healthcare systems can also differ in whether the range of services provided are limited or comprehensive, otherwise known as the difference between basic and extended coverage. In Social Insurance-based systems, supplementary coverage can be obtained from a public insurer or from private insurers. In Social Welfare-based systems, supplementary coverage is usually for complementary services, such as single hospital rooms.

3.4 ADMINISTRATION

In Social Insurance-based systems, the insurer often operates at arm's length from the government. The role of the national or regional government is as a regulator and legislator which sets the general laws governing the healthcare system. In contrast, in Social Welfare-based systems, there is no separate insurer. The role of insurer is assumed by a department of the government, for example, the Department of Health, in the UK.

3.5 DEFINITIONS OF PRIVATE AND PUBLIC HEALTHCARE

According to Saltman (2003), the debate in many European countries regarding privatization suffers from a lack of information regarding how key issues of public and private healthcare have been handled in the past, and how traditional boundaries between the public and private sectors are beginning to fade away in a number of countries. In terms of private healthcare, Saltman distinguishes between the *For Profit* sector which can be provided by small business or large corporations and the *Not for Profit* sector which is provided by Community Based, Religious, Charitable or other NGOs. In particular the emphasis is on the ownership of assets: the private-sector healthcare implies private ownership – that is, non-state ownership – of the assets involved in the delivery of healthcare.[13] In terms of the public healthcare sector, Saltman distinguishes between *the State* sector, which is usually a means federal ownership of assets, and the *Public but Non State* sector, which includes regional and local government and public corporations. Examples of *Public but Non-State* organizations include the County Councils of Sweden, hospital trusts in the UK and independently managed hospitals as well as primary health centres in Sweden.[14]

According to Saltman, the boundaries between these categories have been blurred in Europe. Past anomalies include general practitioners in the UK who are entirely in the private sector, but have received public pensions funded jointly with the state since the NHS was established. In Germany, the statutory sickness funds are technically private not-for-profit organizations, but are administered not under private but under public law. Disputes between subscribers and their sickness fund are resolved by social courts using public sector administrative criteria.[15]

In the next section, a brief overview of the health systems of the UK, France, Belgium, Germany, Sweden and Australia is provided. As will be seen, there is a remarkable variation in the role played by the private sector in the healthcare systems of these countries.

Table 1: Selected Summary Statistics: Healthcare Systems in Selected OECD Countries

	Year		Australia	Belgium	Canada	France	Germany	Sweden	UK	US	
1 Total Expenditure on Health (% GDP)	2001	Total	9.1	9	9.4	9.4	10.8	8.8	7.5	13.9	
		Rank – 1 highest	4	5	3	3	2	6	7	1	
2 Private Expenditure (% total exp. on health)	2001	Total	31.8	28.6	29.9	24.1	21.4	15.1	17	55.1	
		Rank – 1 highest	2	4	3	5	6	8	7	1	
3 Life Expectancy (Total Population at Birth)	2001	Total	79.7	78	79.7	79.2	78.5	79.9	78.1	77.1	
		Rank – 1 highest	2	6	2	3	4	1	5	7	
4 Age Dependency Ratio Pop (0-19)+65+/pop (20-64)	2002	Total	49.1	52.5	45.3	53.7	48	54.5	52.6	50.1	
		Rank – 1 highest	6	4	8	2	7	1	3	5	
5 Practicing Physicians (Density/1000 Population)	2000	Total	2.5	3.9	2.1	3.3	3.3	3	2	2.2	
		Rank – 1 highest	4	1	6	2	2	3	7	5	
6 Practicing Specialists (Density/1000 Population)	2000	Total	1.1	1.8	1.1	1.7	2.2	2.2	1.4	1.4	
		Rank – 1 highest	5	2	5	3	1	1	4	4	
7 MRI units (Number/Population)	1995	Total	2.9	3.3	1.3	2.1	2.3	6.8	3.4	7.2	
		Rank – 1 highest	5	4	8	7	6	2	3	1	
8 Comput. Tomog. Scanners (Number/Population)	1994	Total	18.4	16.7	7.7	8.5	8.6	13.8[a]	6.3[a]	14.9	[a]1993 data
		Rank – 1 highest	1	2	7	6	5	4	8	3	
9 Total In-patient care beds † (/1000 population)	1997	Total	8.3	7.3	4.4	8.6	9.4	4	4.4	3.9	
		Rank – 1 highest	3	4	5	2	1	6	5	7	
10 Admissions: in patient † (/100,000 population)	1997	Total	16300	20000	9710	23100	20026	18100[b]	15052	12558	[b]1996 data
		Rank – 1 highest	5	3	8	1	2	4	6	7	
11 Healthcare Coverage (% of population)	2001	Total	100	99	100	99.9	90.9	100	100	45 †	
		Rank – 1 highest	1	3	1	2	4	1	1	5	
12 Pharmaceutical Coverage (% of population)	2002	Total	100	94	50	99.9	90.9	100	100	12 †	
		Rank – 1 highest	1	3	5	2	4	1	1	6	

Source: OECD Health Data 2004
† OECD Health Data 2001

CHAPTER IV

AN OVERVIEW OF THE HEALTHCARE SYSTEMS OF SELECTED OECD COUNTRIES

4.1 THE UK HEALTHCARE SYSTEM

According to Doyal and Doyal (1999), the growing debate about the inadequacies of the UK healthcare system peaked after the Second World War. Expectations developed among British men and women that appropriate healthcare was part of those basic needs that governments should provide. This expectation was central to the Beveridge Report, which outlined the basic structure of the British welfare state, including the creation of the NHS in 1948. It has been argued that from the very beginning, the NHS required more resources than politicians were willing to provide.[16]

Prior to recent reforms, observers described the NHS (the National Health Service) as the most highly centralized healthcare system in the OECD.[17] The NHS was always a key element of the central government through the Secretary of State, who was accountable to Parliament for all NHS policy and expenditure. Although day-to-day administration was delegated to regional and local bodies, those bodies were appointed by and accountable to the central government. This centralized control by the national government was a key objective of the architects of the NHS. For instance, the creator of the NHS, Aneurin Bevan, was quoted as saying, "when a bedpan is dropped on a hospital floor, its noise should resound in the Palace of Westminster."[18]

Regional budgets were drawn up on a per-capita basis and were passed on to hospitals and other facilities via district health authorities (DHAs), who then used the money to finance hospital and community health services under their administration. General Practitioners were paid through a central contract involving a mixture of capitation, fee-for-service and other payments, administered by local family health service authorities.[19] According to one view, the "command-and-control system of the NHS lacked flexibility, incentives for efficiency, financial information (and hence accountability) and choice of providers of secondary care."[20]

Reforms to the UK Healthcare System have been described as a "case study in the complex process of introducing planned market mechanisms into a command-and-control health system."[21] In order to mimic the private sector, the 1983 Griffiths Report urged the adoption of a more business-like model for the delivery of health services based on a regional rather than national model. For example, the general managers of the regional districts would be hired on short-term contracts and rewarded based on performance. The goal was to presumably align the incentives of managers with the goals of the NHS.

Given the election of the Conservative Party in the 1980's, and the emerging problems in the National Health Service (NHS), a number of proposals for reform were presented in the 1989 white paper entitled *Working for Patients*. The thrust of the proposals was to mimic market-oriented incentives among hospitals and hospital administrators. According to Saltman and von Otter (1992), the actual implementation of the *White Paper* was less dependent upon market mechanisms than originally proposed.

The debate regarding the role of the private sector ranged from a modest inclusion of market incentives to a complete adoption of the insurance-based United States type system. Influential at the time was the 1985 report for the NHS by Alain Enthoven, which advocated an "internal market." In an essay "meant to be a sympathetic review of some problems of organization and management in the National Health Service (NHS) with particular focus on incentives for efficiency and innovation", Enthoven concluded the following:[22]

- The NHS enjoys widespread support in Britain, and it produces a great deal of care for the money spent. But given the tight limits under which it must operate, the NHS will find it increasingly difficult to meet the demands placed upon it.

- The NHS is caught in a 'gridlock' of forces that make change exceedingly difficult to bring about. Public policy should seek to create an environment for the NHS that is hospitable to quality-improving and efficiency-improving change. Opportunities for constructive change should be nurtured, not politicized or other otherwise abused.

- The NHS runs on the ability and dedication of the many people who work in it. But its structure contains no serious incentives to guide the NHS in the direction of better quality care and service at reduced cost. In fact, the structure of the NHS contains perverse incentives.

- The NHS purchasing of acute care services from the private sector now appears to be a matter of 'targets of opportunity'. The NHS doesn't know its own costs and so it isn't able to recognize a good deal when it sees one. Cost-finding systems ought to be developed. The NHS ought to be willing to buy acute care services from the private sector when it can get them at a lower price than the internal cost of providing the services.[23] The NHS could become more of a discerning purchaser of services from competing private suppliers and thereby realize some of the benefits of efficiency and innovation that competition in the private sector offers.

The preceding observations lead Enthoven to recommend an 'Internal Market Model' for the NHS. Each district would receive a per capita revenue and capital allowance. Each district would resemble a nationalized company, responsible for providing and paying for care for its own resident population, and would buy and sell services from and to other Districts and trade with the private sector.[24] In such a scheme, District managers would be free to use all their resources most efficiently. While some perverse incentives would be eliminated, the main defect would be a lack of powerful incentives for NHS personnel to serve patients as efficiently as possible. Enthoven's overall view is that "the principle that the government will make comprehensive health services freely available to all does not mean that the governments must produce them itself."[25]

(a) Financing

As of 1996-97, NHS was predominantly financed by general taxes (81.5%), along with additional payments of social premiums, termed (NI or national insurance contributions) (12.2%). The remaining (6.3%) came from user charges (2.1%) repayment of NHS trust interest-bearing debt (3.0%), and other miscellaneous sources (1.2%).[26] It has been argued that NI contributions are tantamount to an income tax.[27]

(b) Changes to the Organization of the NHS

A number of NHS reforms emerged out of *Working for Patients*, introduced in 1989. According to West (1998:168), the NHS reforms were designed to introduce market forces and competition as a means of increasing the efficiency of public healthcare. The idea was to have District Health Authorities (DHAs) become purchasers of healthcare for defined resident populations. DHAs could buy services through contracts with local or distant health service providers, termed NHS trusts, but also from private sector providers. This has been termed a purchaser/provider split.

General Practitioners, who are the primary care providers of the NHS, were also given the opportunity to become purchasers, along with the right to hold the purchasing budget for elective (non-emergency) hospital care if they so desired.[28] GP fund-holding involved the management of a budget for the GP's own practice, including staff, certain hospital referrals, drug costs, community nursing services and management costs. By 1996, GP fund-holding, involved over half the population for non-emergency service.[29]

In some cases groups of GP fundholders agreed to pool their budgets and work together in what were called Multifunds. Apart from GP fundholders and Multifunds, other organizational bodies also developed, including NHS trusts, which are public bodies providing NHS hospital and community healthcare. The White Paper, *The New NHS*, (December 1997), called for a drastic change in the structure of the NHS. Prior to the White Paper the financing and accountability arrangements in the NHS called for the 3,500 GP fundholders (involving 15,000 GPs) and 100 Health Authorities to be accountable to the Regional Offices of the NHS Executive. In turn, 80 TPPs (involving 1,500 GPs) and a number of Commissioning Groups (involving 7,000 GPs) were accountable to the 100 Health Authorities.[30] The TPPs were an NHS Executive initiative created in 1993, to extend the fundholding scheme. These "total purchasing pilots" have been described as a situation in which GPs in a locality would purchase all hospital and community health services for their patients.[31] As well 450 NHS Trusts and 100 Multifunds (involving 2,600 GPs) were accountable directly to the Regional Offices. In terms of contractual arrangements, all the above (apart from the regional offices) had contracts with the NHS trusts.

Enthoven (2000), in reviewing the experiment with internal markets, cites the review by Julian Legrand (1998), who found that post-reform NHS activity rose faster than resources. This implies an increase in efficiency attributable to the reforms. However, they also concluded that measurable changes were not as great as was predicted, attributable to the fact that the essential conditions required for a market to operate were not fulfilled.[32]

(c) Recent Developments

The most recent government position on the NHS is contained in *The NHS Plan (2000)*, presented to Parliament by the Secretary for Health, July 2000. In the Executive summary, the NHS is described as "a 1940's system operating in a 21st century world."[33] The report states that the NHS suffers from a lack of national standards, old-fashioned demarcations between staff and barriers between services, the absence of clear incentives and levers to improve performance, and over-centralization and disempowered patients.

The Plan lists the 10 core principles of the NHS:

1. The NHS will provide a universal service for all based on clinical need, not ability to pay.
2. The NHS will provide a comprehensive range of services.
3. The NHS will shape its services around the needs and preferences of individual patients, their families and their careers.
4. The NHS will respond to different needs of different populations.
5. The NHS will work continuously to improve quality services and to minimise errors.
6. The NHS will support and value its staff.
7. Public funds for Healthcare will be devoted solely to NHS patients.
8. The NHS will work together with others to ensure a seamless service for patients.
9. The NHS will help keep people healthy and work to reduce health inequalities.
10. The NHS will respect the confidentiality of individual patients and provide open access to information about services, treatment and performance

Most of these principles are self-explanatory. However, a few require elaboration. Principle 4 implies that while health services will continue to be funded nationally, and available to all citizens of the UK, some regional variation is to be expected. However, the goal is to reduce unjustified variations and raise standards to achieve a truly National Health Service. Principle 7 states while the NHS will continue to be funded out of public expenditure, primarily taxation, "individuals will remain free to spend their own money as they see fit, but public funds will be devoted solely to NHS patients, and not be used to subsidize individuals' privately funded healthcare."[34]

To accomplish the listed changes, the March 2000 budget meant that the NHS will grow by one half in cash terms, and by one third in real terms in just 5 years.

(d) Changes in the Relationship between the NHS and the private sector

The *NHS Plan (2000)* discusses a number of issues regarding the present and proposed future relationship of the NHS to the private sector. Among the points the *Plan* authors make are:

- Using extra capacity and extra investment from voluntary and private sector providers can benefit NHS patients. In particular, it observes that "The Private Finance Initiative is already delivering new hospitals, on time, to budget as part of the biggest hospital building programme in the history of the NHS."[35]

- The NHS already spends over £1 billion each year on buying care and specialist services from hospitals, nursing homes and hospices run by private companies and charities.[36]

It is interesting to further outline the thinking of Plan authors' about the new relationship.[37]

> "For decades there has been a stand-off between the NHS and the private sector providers of Healthcare. This has to end. Ideological boundaries or institutional barriers should not stand in the way of better care for NHS patients. Public funding for the NHS will increase substantially over the next four years. The private and voluntary sectors have a role to play in ensuring that NHS patients get the full benefit from this extra investment. By constructing the right partnerships the NHS can harness the capacity of private and voluntary providers to treat more NHS patients."

> "Developing these new forms of partnership will not compromise the fundamental principles underpinning this Plan: that Healthcare should be available on the basis of need, not ability to pay. There is a world of difference between the NHS paying to have patients treated, as NHS patients, in a private hospital for free, and what some propose – forcing patients out of the NHS to pay for their own care. Under our proposals a

patient would remain an NHS patient even if they were treated in the private sector. NHS care will remain free at the point of delivery, whether care is provided by an NHS hospital, a local GP, a private sector hospital or by a voluntary organization."

(e) Role of the Private Sector

According to Calnan, Cant and Gabe (1993) "since the inception of the NHS there has always been a private health sector in the United Kingdom, although its size has varied according to political economic and social circumstances."[38] The role of the private sector, it has been suggested, was a result of a political compromise. In return for accepting salaries (for work in hospitals) and capitation fees (for general practice), doctors would be allowed to continue their private practice for a fixed proportion of their time.[39]

A. Concordat

Perhaps the most significant recent change in the structure of the UK health system is the concordat signed between the Independent Sector and the Department of Health in 2000. The Concordat is a letter of understanding which clarifies the role of the private healthcare sector in the UK health system. Among the key elements of the Concordat are the following:

> "There should be no organizational or ideological barriers to the delivery of high quality healthcare free at the point of delivery to those who need it, when they need it...The (Concordat) describes a partnership approach that enables NHS patients in England to be treated free in the private and voluntary healthcare sector."

> "The key tests for any relationship between the NHS and private and voluntary healthcare providers is that it must represent good value for money for the tax payer and assure high standards of care for the patient."

> The concordat focuses initially on three areas, 1) elective care, 2) critical care and 3) intermediate care facilities.

The concordat is described as an enabling framework in which the detailed decisions and arrangements are to be made locally. The concordat offers examples of the types of cooperative arrangements that might be pursued. For elective care, Primary Care Groups or Primary

Care Trusts might commission or rent accommodation from the private and voluntary-care sector, with the service delivered by NHS consultants and other NHS staff under their NHS contract. Alternatively, an NHS Trust might subcontract for the provision of a service to the private and voluntary healthcare provider. The NHS Trust would receive resources from the PCG/PCT under a service agreement between the Trust and the PCG/PCT. Finally, Primary Care Groups or Primary Care Trusts might directly commission a private and voluntary healthcare provider. According to Saltman, "these PCTs represent a new public-private hybrid, which is considerably more publicly accountable than the immediate (private for-profit) fund-holding predecessor model."[40] That is, the Primary Care Groups in the UK require private GPs who contract with the NHS to work in large group practices designed and closely regulated by the state through the NHS Executive.

B. The Independent Hospital Sector

Hospital services provided outside the NHS come under the rubric of the Independent Hospital Sector. As of 1994, 20% of all elective surgical operations, and 30% of all hip replacements took place in the independent sector.[41] As of 1998, there were 229 independent medical/surgical hospitals in the UK with operating theatres registered to take inpatients; their beds totalled 10,852. The independent hospital sector is dominated by four main hospital chains or operators: (1) BMI Healthcare – 40 hospitals, 20.7% of the total number of beds in the independent sector; (2) BUPA Health Services – 36 hospitals, 17.1% of beds; (3) Nuffield Hosptials – 38 hospitals, 14.3% of beds; (4) Community Hospitals Group PLC – 22 hospitals, 7.6 % of beds. Together they account for approximately 60% of the total number of hospitals, and approximately the same share of beds.

C. Working in both the public and private sector

A somewhat unique arrangement exists within the UK health system which has consultants (specialists) working both within the NHS and in private clinics or in the private wings of NHS hospitals. With respective to NHS consultants, the Review Body on Doctors' and Dentists' Remuneration (DDRB), established in 1963, recommends the basic salary for a whole-time consultant (currently £66,120) at the maximum, as well as the levels and numbers of distinction awards payable to consultants.[42] The contract for the whole-time consultant is based on the equivalent of 35 hours per week, which is equal to 10 notional half days flexibly worked.[43] Consultants who are classified as whole-time consultants are restricted to earning 10% of gross NHS remuneration from private practice. Those wishing to earn more must give up some of their NHS earnings to do so, with the most common arrangement, described as a maximum part-time consultant, is for consultants to give up one eleventh of their NHS pay to have the freedom to earn income above the 10% limit from private practice. These maximum part time consultants are expected to deliver the same amount of NHS work as their whole time counterparts.[44]

According to Nicholson (1998), doctors and other medical staff practice have practiced privately in addition to their NHS work for as long as the NHS has existed. He argues that this has allowed them to supplement their income, and continue to work with the NHS at salary levels that the public sector can afford.[45]

D. *Private Insurance*

There is extensive private insurance in the UK health system, which takes mainly two forms, employment or company-based insurance (representing 59% of the total) and individual insurance (making up 31%). The remaining 10% is made up of voluntary employee-paid groups, based on professional associations or trade unions, with employees paying the costs of premiums themselves.[46] As of 1996, 10.8% of the population in the UK was covered by private health insurance, which is used mainly to cover the costs of acute healthcare.[47] As of 1995, the socioeconomic groups that have the largest shares of private insurance were (1) professional, 20% for the 16-44 age group and 23% for the 45-64 age group and (2) employers and managers, 23% for the 16-44 age group and 26% for 45-64 age group. After that age the rates drop significantly for the employer and manager group but less so for the professional class.

Private insurance is both of a complementary nature, much like Blue Cross coverage in Canada for a hospital room with one or two patients, and also offers what might be viewed as improved access. It is generally agreed that private patients get quicker treatment for elective surgery, which is paid for by insurance coverage. The type of insurance coverage sought seems to be mostly of a fixed payout nature, that is, the contract with the insurance agency calls for a fixed total payout if a particular medical service is required. The alternative– full coverage of hospital or physician costs– seems to be a small and declining share of the market.

E. *Private Financing of Hospitals*

The Private Finance Initiative (PFI) is a program whereby private capital finances the construction of hospitals on contract with the NHS, subject to the specifications requested by the Regional Offices of the NHS. The contract calls for a payment from the NHS to the private investors to cover the costs of capital for the project. Once the agreed-upon payment schedule is completed, the hospital ownership reverts to the NHS. Positions on the efficacy of these contracts vary, with strong support found within the NHS, and some concern expressed by the British Medical Association.

F. *Contracts for Doctors*

Currently most specialists in the UK are employees of the NHS and are paid a salary.[48] The consultants, and hence their pay, are differentiated by grade.

General Practitioners are also paid a salary but additional expenses are directly reimbursed by the NHS for staff, premises and information technology. According to the BMA, general practitioners currently incur expenses at 60% of turnover which they acknowledge is high by professional standards. Furthermore, both consultants and general practitioners, given their employment status, are eligible to receive pensions.

Recently, the issue of self-employment status for consultants has been raised, because "in particular there is now increasing acceptance, indeed promotion, of a role for the private sector in [the] finance, delivery and management [of Healthcare]."[49] According to the BMA "unsurprisingly and as a result, there has been renewed interest by doctors in other forms of contractual relationship with the NHS. In particular, consultants are attracted by the status of free standing practitioner providing services to the NHS on a fee for service basis."[50]

In the discussion of a change in the employment status of consultants (who would be termed specialists), a number of issues arise. These include 1) contractual relationships as well as hospital admission privileges, 2) hospital payment versus patient payment, 3) market rates versus fee schedules, 4) professional expenses, 5) pension issues, 6) income variability by specialty and 7) organizational issues and quality of service control. Most of these issues are addressed and managed to a certain extent where fee-for-service prevails, but they become quite significant when moving from a salary compensation scheme.

4.2 THE FRENCH HEALTHCARE SYSTEM

Some observers argue that the French healthcare system has been overlooked in comparative studies. This is surprising since according to Rodwin and Sandier (1993), it has many elements that appeal to supporters of an increased role for the market, including "fee-for-service reimbursement, total freedom of provider choice, an important private for-profit hospital sector, and patient copayments."[51] This is in a system that spent 9.4% of its gross domestic product (GDP) on healthcare in 1998, similar to Canada (9.3%) and but less that the US (12.9%) (see Table 6.)

The French system moreover

> ...provides almost universal coverage with a uniform comprehensive benefit plan that, unlike those in the United States, includes pharmaceuticals, physical therapy, and even medically prescribed spa treatments. Consumers have coverage that follows them from job to job, including any intervening periods of unemployment. Out-of-pocket costs are capped below the level where they could cause financial hardship. There is free choice of office-based physicians and ancillary service provides for ambulatory care.[52]

A key feature of the French system is the twin elements of freedom of choice and almost universal coverage. The freedom of choice relates to the sizable presence of a private sector in healthcare in which "private hospital care accounted for 24.2% of total hospital expenses but over two fifths of patient days in short stay hospitals."[53] The private facilities evolved from *cliniques*, for-profit doctors' hospitals. These facilities are most often used for routine operations, maternity care, and care for particular categories of problems such as cancer.[54]

The French system, involving as it does the public/private mix in the financing and provision of healthcare, rests, according to Rodwin and Sandier, "on the principle of pluralism – the tolerance of some organizational diversity, whether it is complementary, competitive or both. With respect to financing, pluralism justifies the coexistence of multiple statutory health insurance schemes, complementary private health insurance coverage, and significant cost sharing directly by patients. With respect to the provision of health services, pluralism justifies the coexistence of public and private hospitals and both office-based private practice and public ambulatory care."[55]

This pluralism coupled with the ideal of *la médecine libérale* (first formulated in 1928 by the principal physician trade union), means that physicians should be free to practice on a fee-for-service basis, and be assured clinical autonomy, whereas patients should be free to choose their physicians (and vice versa). As well, direct payments should be made between patients and doctors in private practice.[56]

The French population is covered by the National Health Insurance – NHI (Assurance Maladie), which is organized along occupational lines.[57] Since 1978, the unemployed have had access to the Social Insurance Funds (SIFs) through individual contributions. Since 1988, local governments have been required to pay the premiums for those without a defined minimum income level on request.[58] In 1990, it was estimated that 350,000 to 500,000 French citizens and other residents were without coverage, which constituted approximately 1% of the population of 56 million.[59] As of 1999, only approximately 300,000 people were uninsured in France (due to homelessness or other socioeconomic problems). Patients pay providers directly when service is provided, and are then reimbursed. Not all the cost is reimbursed, however, since patients pay what is called a ticket modérateur either directly through out of pocket payment or through complementary (additional) insurance.

There are a number of unique features of the French healthcare system.[60] One is that everybody in France over the age of 16 keeps their own medical records, which is presented when treatment is sought. Given that these records are in hard copy, there is a desire to introduce a more efficient method of record keeping. France has introduced an electronic card, SESAM-Vitale, which has a patient's medical recorded encoded. Apart from the advantages for physicians, the information can be used for statistical purposes.[61]

The Medical Control Service assumes an important role in the French health-care system, having monitored the delivery of healthcare since 1945. Originally recruited by treasuries and placed under their authority, the "advising practitioners" have since 1967 been working independently. They receive a salary from CNAMTS – which is the insurance program for salaried workers and their dependents – and are regularly registered with a chapter of their Professional Order. It is important to note that all practitioners – doctor, dental surgeon, or pharmacist – have the right to apply for a position. As of 1999, the Medical Control Service consisted of 2,600 advising practitioners, who were assisted by 7,800 administrative officials. The Medical Control Service has four missions: 1) to control and justify the granting of medical benefits, 2) to control for abuse of the patients, 3) to ensure that justifiable payments are made – for example, ensuring that insurance companies pay hospitals for justifiable claims, and 4) to analyze the activity of health professionals, to ensure that health professionals adhere to legislation and its regulations.[62] The Medical Control Service is also an important contributor to the overall planning of the healthcare system based on information it obtains from the evaluation processes undertaken by hospital establishments and health insurance firms. The Service also controls how the private establishments are run.

(a) Financing

The French system exhibits a public/private mix in both the financing and provision of services, with a strong government role to ensure universal coverage and to regulate the health system.[63] The Securité Sociale (through the sickness funds) finances 73.9% of the healthcare expenditures, patients incur 13.8% and while complementary funds (mutuelles and private insurance companies) cover 7%.[64] The amount financed by the social security system is funded by compulsory contributions related to income shared between employers (70%) and employees (30%).[65]

To finance the benefits under the French national insurance for the 80 percent of the population covered by CNAMTS requires that employers pay 12.8 percent of the wage bill, while employees contribute 6.9 percent of their full salary, amounting to a total payroll tax for health insurance of 19.7 percent of all wages.[66]

(b) The Role of the Private Sector

Complementary insurance is held by 87% of the population in France; it is purchased from private nonprofit mutuelles (supplementary insurance funds) or from for-profit insurance companies.[67] The latter cover legal liability for contributions and also cover risks not included within the health-insurance system. According to Fielding and Lancry, "supplemental insurance has benefitted from the consistent support of the government, which wishes to reduce pressure on it to increase employer and employee contributions to keep up with healthcare cost increases."[68]

French physicians and other health professionals in private practice are paid directly by patients on a fee-for-service basis. Physicians in general and family practice make up 53% of all physicians in office based private practice in France, compared to 16% in the U.S.[69]

From 1980 to 1990, the French government allowed any physician to enroll in a second tier of physicians, which had the effect of allowing those physicians to charge 1.5 times the nationally negotiated rates.[70] By permitting these physicians to opt out, "the government and SIF (Sickness Insurance Funds) could respond to physician complaints of being grossly under-remunerated without agreeing to increases in SIFs' fee schedules."[71] In 1989 the average French physician earned the US equivalent of $45,000 net, while German physicians earned $77,000 (in 1988) in comparison to the average of $156,000 for a US physician. In terms of gross revenue, French specialists grossed about $180,000 US while French generalists grossed an average of $100,000 US.[72] By 1991, tier-two physicians comprised more than 26% of all physicians, including 34% of specialists but only 15% of generalists.

According to Rodwin and Sandier, "French public and private hospitals differ in mission, technical level of medical services, patient clientele, mode of reimbursement under national health insurance, and teaching autonomy."[73] Regional public hospitals affiliated with medical schools emphasize teaching and research. These hospitals generally offer the most sophisticated high-technology procedures. Public hospitals must accept all patients and provide emergency care. According to Rodwin and Sandier, "although public and private hospitals serve a cross-section of the population, the poor are more likely to receive care in a public hospital."[74]

Table 1 provides some data on hospitals in France, with two types of private hospital types listed, those subscribing to the qualified national target (OQN) and those that do not.[75] The private sector has 59 percent of all short-stay hospital beds in France, 68% of all surgical beds, 47 percent of all psychiatric beds and 46 percent of all medical beds. The *Cliniques* concentrate on elective surgery and obstetrics, with more complex cases left to the public sector.

Table 2: Hospitals in France (Selected Statistics)

Area		Public Hospitals		Private not under OQN		Private Hosp. Under OQN		Total
Medicine								
– Number of hospitals	(%)	751	(54%)	177	(13%)	465	(33%)	1393
– Beds		94,897		10,296		14,119		119,312
– Admissions (1,000s)		4,239.0		398.5		681.9		5319.4
Surgery								
– Number of hospitals	(%)	399	(32%)	118	(9%)	740	(59%)	1257
– Beds		48,043		8,675		47,889		104,607
– Admissions (1,000s)		2,295.8		369.2		2697.2		
Obstetrics								
– Number of hospitals	(%)	382	(52%)	47	(6%)	305	(42%)	734
– Beds		15,083		1,479		8,491		25,053
– Admissions (1,000s)		797.7		77.3		414.9		1289.9
Short Term								
– Number of hospitals	(%)	753	(41%)	200	(11%)	871	(48%)	1824
– Beds		158,023		20,450		70,499		248,972
– Admissions (1,000s)		7,332.6		845.1		3794.1		11,971.8
Psychiatric								
– Number of hospitals	(%)	240	(53%)	85	(18%)	132	(29%)	457
– Beds		46,030		11,116		10,332		67,478
– Admissions (1,000s)		418.9		67.2		102.9		589
Drug and alcohol addiction								
– Number of hospitals	(%)	66	(78%)	13	(15%)	6	(7%)	85
– Beds		1,174		367		271		1812
– Admissions (1,000s)		17.1		3.0		3.9		24
Aftercare and rehabilitation								
– Number of hospitals	(%)	745	(47%)	461	(29%)	387	(24%)	1593
– Beds		38,287		30,722		22,329		91,338
– Admissions (1,000s)		366.2		260.3		229.0		855.5
Long term Care								
– Number of hospitals	(%)	859	(87%)	119	(12%)	8	(1%)	986
– Beds		75,273		6,820		341		82,434
– Admissions (1,000s)		51.9		4.9		.33		57.1
Total								
– Number of hospitals	(%)	1042	(33%)	745	(24%)	1333	(43%)	3120
– Beds		318,787		69,475		103,772		492,034
– Admissions (1,000s)		8,186.9		1,180.6		4,130.3		13,479.8

Source: SAE 1998 – reported in European Union of Independent Hospitals 2001.

The *Cliniques* as well as private nonprofit hospitals are paid directly by the national health insurance funds on the basis of a negotiated daily charge and a fee schedule for hospital-specific charges for such services as the use of an operating room.

The remaining balance – a 20 percent copayment for the daily charge – is recovered directly by *cliniques* from patients. Physicians in *cliniques*, as in private practice, typically bill their patients directly; patients in turn are reimbursed according to the charges of the national fee schedule. (R&S, 119).

(c) Recent Developments[76]

France has been experimenting with a number of reforms in the 1990's. For example, the government of former Prime Minister Alain Juppe passed a plan in 1995 that would include a special tax on all incomes, as well as a number of plans to streamline health administration in a thorough reform of the social security system.

Key measures included an extra 0.5% tax on income, including savings and social benefits, and a vote on an annual budget for the social security's health insurance branch. The latter was seen as a check on the powers of the fund, which was largely controlled by employers and trade unions. Other measures involved a role for regional agencies to allocate hospital budgets to private and public hospitals based on need and quality and cost criteria. In addition, the number of hospital beds would be gradually reduced. In a historic change, patients will be now encouraged to consult a general practitioner rather than a specialist.[77]

In October 1996, additional measures to reduce the huge deficit in the social security system, which provides health insurance, retirement, maternity and other benefits, were introduced. The deficit has been traced to slow economic growth and high unemployment rather than increased health spending. The measures include increased taxes on alcohol, and authorization for pharmacists to substitute generic drugs in place of brand name drugs subscribed by doctors.[78]

Subsequent reforms met with considerable resistance from healthcare professionals in the following year. Medical interns went on strike, later to be joined by many hospital department heads. They were protesting the government's plan to control the deficit in healthcare spending by imposing fines on doctors if the maximum level of spending determined by parliament was exceeded. The fines amount to as much as Fr. 14 400 (£1550; $2,480) a year.[79] The imposition of a system of collective fines for doctors if their health spending exceeded the annual amount was determined unconstitutional in 1999. It was considered unconstitutional because the collective sanctions penalize not only those doctors who overspent but also doctors who may not have done so.[80]

The Socialist government of Lionel Jospin, having replaced the Conservative government of Alain Juppe, nevertheless shared the former government's concern with rising health insurance costs. The reforms were sweeping and included a significant change in the financing of the social security system and its national health insurance plan. The most notable change was a shift of the base of contributions for employees from 5.5% of gross salary to a contribution rate of 0.75%, with the loss in revenues being made up with a tax of 4.1% on all income including retirement pensions, interest on savings, and capital gains. The employer's share remains twice the original contribution rate of 5.5%, and the increase in the tax rate of 4.1%, when coupled with earlier increases to this levy, results in a tax on most incomes at a rate of 7.5%.[81]

In February 1998, the French government announced that a bonus was to be awarded to each GP of Fr. 9 300 (£930; $1,500) because health spending by GPs was under budget. Specialists exceeded their budget and received no bonus. The trade unions for GPs were split regarding the desirability of the bonus, with views ranging from support for a well deserved bonus, to concern that the bonus would alter the doctor-patient relationship and its acceptance would be condoning the principle of controlled health expenditures.[82]

A significant reform involves moving the GP to a Gatekeeper role. First proposed in the Juppé plan, the change is to have patients subscribe to a single general practitioner for treatment and only consult another practitioner in case of emergency or during travel. If deemed necessary, patients would then be referred to a specialist. In 1998, a four year agreement was struck between the "Sécu" and the General Practitioner union (Médecins Généralistes France). Under the agreement, the patient will pay nothing directly to the doctor, with the doctor being paid a lump sum for each subscriber and an agreed fee for each patient visit by the "Sécu". In addition subscribed doctors were not to exceed a limit of 7500 consultations a year. The system was opposed by three other unions of general practitioners, as well as specialists who would only see patients by referral. Both groups threatened job action.[83] A survey of France's main medical association of more than 6200 doctors showed 58% in opposition to the new system based on limitations on patients' freedom to choose, 38% resented the financial penalties, 60% feared a reduction in the quality of healthcare, and 67% worried about the loss of income.[84]

The reforms have been felt in a number of areas in the French healthcare system. Massive demonstrations occurred in February 2000, to protest staff shortages and health budget restrictions imposed by government. The reforms have led to a significant reduction in the number of hospital beds and the number of hospital staff. Most hospital administrators complain of a large number of hospital positions being unfilled or being replaced by temporary staff at lower salaries than French colleagues, shortages of nurses and increased waiting lists. Increased percentages of young medical graduates are choosing private practice, with 80% making the decision in 1998.[85]

An additional plank in the reform proposals was the ability of the government, since May 2000, to limit the fee charged by GPs and specialists if the expenditure by one speciality was deemed excessive. For example, fees for various radiological procedures were decreased by an average of 13.5% because spending in the discipline exceeded the limit set by parliament.[86]

As of September 2000, French healthcare costs were still rising rapidly. Highest increases were recorded for private practice, costs of prescribed pharmaceuticals, and payments to patients on sick leave from work. Public officials felt that this was only a transitional increase given that negotiated agreements with the medical profession were being tested.[87]

4.3 THE GERMAN HEALTHCARE SYSTEM

The German Healthcare system has its origins in self-help or mutual aid societies which were originally designed to provide insurance to cover health risks related to employment. Gradually, they evolved into a system of general health coverage. As part of the German social security system, healthcare is said to be based on the principles of solidarity and subsidiarity.[88]

The catalogue of benefits are contained in the Social Code Book V, which is federal legislation. The Code Book guarantees the insured coverage that is sufficient, necessary, useful and economic.[89] The Basic Elements and Characteristics of the German Healthcare System have been described as (i) solidarity, (ii) self-government, (iii) contribution financed, (iv) comprehensive coverage, (v) branched social insurance system, (vi) benefit-in-kind principle. One characterization of Solidarity in the context of the German healthcare system "is a sharing of health risks among the population insured. Solidarity also means that contributions should rise in line with ability to pay."[90] The principle of subsidiarity implies that "the state should not assume any functions which the individual, the family or private self-organization could solve better or at least equally well by their own efforts and on their own responsibility."[91]

(a) Financing

Almost 90% of the German population is insured by one of the 754 sickness funds (SHIs), which are self-governing, self-sustaining and self-financing institutions.[92] The contribution rate for the sickness funds is determined by an elected board of directors who are representatives of the insured members and the employers.

Membership in an SHI or an alternative health insurance fund is compulsory for German citizens. The compulsory aspect is enforced much along the lines of the compulsory payments for Employment Insurance and Old Age Security in the Canadian social-security system. Employees must inform employers of the particular SHI with which they are registered, since the employer must send its share of the employee's premiums to the particular fund. For individuals who are unemployed there is a special fund, financed by the state, and dedicated to covering the medical costs of those not covered through employment.

The contributions to the SHI are 50% financed by employers and employees. The payroll deduction rate is the same for all fund members regardless of risk characteristics such as, age, sex, individual health risk and number of dependents. Spouses and family dependents up to 18 years are automatically covered if they earn less than a minimum threshold. Hospitals receive a budget from the SHI which is based on DRGs (Diagnostic Related Groups) lump-sum basic costs. Physicians employed in hospitals are salaried, while other physicians not in hospitals are self-employed.[93] According to Kamke (1998:171), "stability of the contribution rate is the uppermost political objective of current healthcare reform initiatives. Options under discussion include reductions in the benefit package and increases in patients' co-payments."

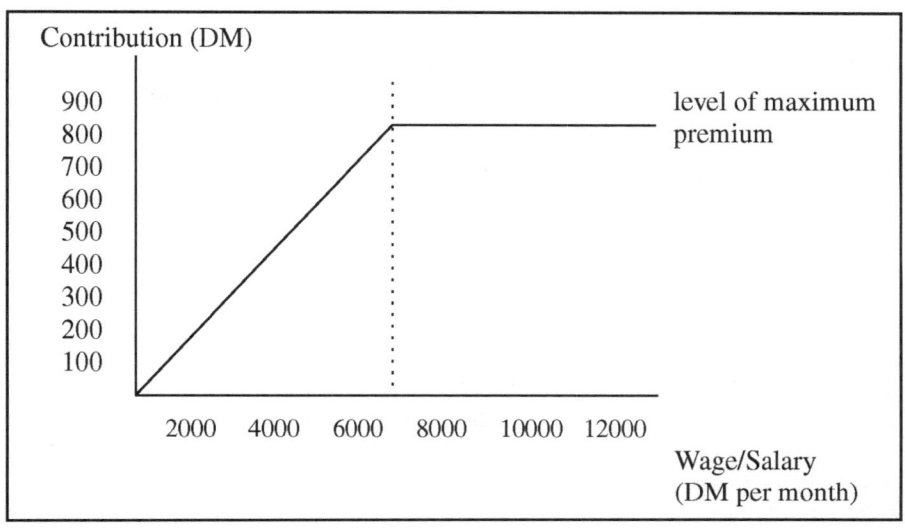

Figure 3: SHI-Contribution
Source: German Medical Association (update 2000)

While civil servants are excluded from the SHI system, the government assists them in obtaining private insurance. As of 1998, 72 million Germans were insured with the SHI system, 7.2 million were covered by Private Insurance, with 7.6 million covered by SHI plus Private Care.[94] The latter is supplementary private insurance for private care for SHI patients. It involves a consultant guarantee, single-room hospital care, and even better hospital food. Apart from the civil servants, other groups with entirely private insurance include patients who have opted out of the SHI system once their income level has exceeded the threshold, as well as self-employed individuals.[95]

There are 52 private health insurers which are represented by the Assembly of Private Health Companies.[96] Apart from these, there are 45 other small and regional private health insurers. Private health premiums vary with age, sex, and medical history. Unlike SHI patients, privately-insured people pay providers directly and are reimbursed by their insurers.

The contributions for an SHI are described by the graph in Figure 3.

Insurance contributions are related to income, but with an upper limit, much like the Employment Insurance contributions in Canada. There is a provision in the German Healthcare system for opting out from the SHI system. The opting out arrangement is once-and-for-all; once the decision is made to opt out it is not possible for the individual to return to the SHI system. The opting out level is 6450 DM of wage/salary per month in the West and 5325 in the East. The upper limit nature of contributions makes the opting out of high income individuals less problematic for the public system, since their contributions are not open ended. If they leave, the public system only loses the maximum required contributions.

An important issue related to sick-fund membership is the competition that exists between funds for members. Beginning in 1996, the Healthcare Structure Act gave almost every insured person the right to change their sickness fund, provided three months notice was given and it was only done once a year.[97] Prior to the implementation of the Act, a risk compensation scheme was introduced to compensate funds for the differences in the in the risk characteristics of their members. The compensation scheme requires all sickness funds to transfer or receive funds based on the differences between their contributory incomes and their estimated expenditure. The estimated expenditure is based on the actual expenditure for both men and women in the previous year.[98] It is felt that the compensation scheme will remain a permanent feature of the German healthcare system.[99]

Some competition does remain between the SHIs, primarily at the level of the premiums charged. The issue of adverse selection arises, with lower risks being attracted to particular funds which have a lower premium due to their healthier risk pool. One issue raised by officials involved in providing SHI insurance services is that the information on the characteristics of individuals within their fund are generally not revealed to SHI fund managers. That is, the insurers lack key information on the nature of their insurees.

It is important to emphasize that the SHIs do not own hospitals or employ physicians or nurses. The financing and provision of health services is based on contracts between the sickness funds and the provider organizations.[100] For example, an interesting feature of the German healthcare system for ambulatory medicine is the role of the Association of Office Physicians (AOP), a self-governing body of physicians. The AOP negotiates with the Sickness Funds (SHI) on a fee schedule for medical services provided by physicians, with contracts negotiated on a Land (regional) basis. To treat SHI patients a physician must have a contract with the AOP. The AOP receives the remuneration from the Sickness Fund and then pays the physicians based on the services provided. The AOP also has a monitoring role regarding physician practice. As of 2000, the federal government has put a cap on the budgets of the AOP.

As of December 31, 1999, there were 292,100 active physicians in Germany. This number can be broken down into hospital employment (47%), ambulatory care (41%), private practice (2%), public health statutory bodies (4%) and other fields (6%).[101] Physicians employed in hospitals are all salaried. Physicians in private practice tend to be retired university-employed physicians who open private practice. In general they don't have a contract with AOP, and so are not allowed to treat SHI patients.

(b) Role of the Private Sector

According to Hinrichs (1995), private sickness funds insure about nine percent of the population. This includes mainly "high-wage earners, self-employed persons and most civil servants (who are reimbursed for parts of their medical expenses by their respective branches of government) and their dependents."[102]

It is instructive to outline the mechanism of service provision in the German system. According to Hinrichs (1995), the relationship is trilateral, involving the sickness fund, the patient, and the private sector. Medical services in the German system are provided by private agencies engaged in ambulatory or hospital care. These agencies contract with the sickness funds to provide healthcare services to their members, with the remuneration the subject of negotiation between the associations of sickness funds and associations of providers.[103]

(c) Recent Developments

The German health system has seen a number of reforms since 1989. The latest was a reaction to the deficit of DM3.5bn ($2.25 bn.) incurred by the public health-insurance system in 1995. The losses were attributed to a combination of increased unemployment (which lowered contributions) and increased healthcare costs. In order to eliminate the deficit it was suggested that health-insurance contributions would have to rise from 13% to 14.2%.[104] The governing party planned to penalize hospitals that exceeded their budgets in order to control increases in hospital costs, which were seen as responsible for a large fraction of the deficit. The longer-range plan was to eliminate economically inefficient hospitals.[105] The healthcare reforms of 1997 did not involve changes to the health-insurance contributions, but did involve an increase in prescription charges and other charges to patients.[106]

A number of recent changes have occurred in the German healthcare system. Perhaps the most significant is the unification of the healthcare systems of the former East and West Germany. The system in East Germany was replaced by the basic elements of the Federal German model in early 1991. The former system of polyclinics and related facilities in the East was allowed to continue for five years after unification. Now, ten years later, the two systems have been described as indistinguishable.[107] After a brief transition in which deaths in the East rose due to the sudden availability of western cars and an increase in homicides, the improvement in health exceeded the most optimistic predictions. Between 1992 and 1997, life expectancy at birth in the former East Germany increased by 2.3 years in males and by 2.4 years in females, higher than increases in Poland, Hungary and West Germany.[108] Credit for the improvement has been given to reduction in deaths due to injuries and violence among young men, as well as an improvement in diet, and a reduction in neonatal mortality due to an improvement in the quality of healthcare.[109]

While currently private hospitals represent a small proportion of German hospitals (concentrating mainly on the care and rehabilitation of chronically ill patients), there is a trend towards the privatisation and closure of state owned hospitals.[110] Table 2 indicates that while the total number of beds in the German hospital system declined by 12%, the number of beds in the private sector increased by 59%. A panel of twenty seven German healthcare experts, asked to forecast the future of the healthcare system predicted a reduction of 25% in the number of German hospitals, with most of them being owned either by private companies or by nonprofit organizations.[111] They predicted that only a few hundred of the current total of 2,258 hospitals would be controlled by the state. Presently private companies, partly sponsored by private health insurance and other investors, are taking over hospitals and introducing modern management and marketing techniques. The privately financed hospitals are in general open to all patients, and not just the 10% of the German population with private health insurance.[112]

Table 3: German Hospitals 1990-1998 (selected statistics)

	Public		Not-for-Profit		Private		Total
	Beds	(%)	Beds	(%)	Beds	(%)	Beds
1990	387,207	(62.8%)	206,936	(33.5%)	22,779	(3.7%)	616,922
1998	295,382	(55.3%)	202,270	(37.9%)	36,118	(6.8%)	533,770
Change		-24%		-2%		59%	-12%

Source: European Observatory on Healthcare Systems, Healthcare Systems in Transition, Germany (2000).

German healthcare officials believe that the relatively high cost attributed to the German system is misleading. They argue that the total expenditure as a fraction of GDP is misleading since unification brought into the German system, a high-cost, low-GDP region, East Germany. It is felt that the recent figure is transitory, because as incomes rise in the East, the denominator will rise and the numerator will be stabilized. Improved economic conditions will also lead to improved health in the former East German.

(d) Comments on the German Healthcare System

The German Healthcare System provides an example of how a private healthcare system can coexist alongside a public system. The German approach is to allow German citizens to opt out of the public system and rely entirely on a private system of healthcare. Healthcare is privately provided and citizens rely on their sickness fund to ensure they receive the needed care. The sickness funds in turn negotiate with the private agencies that provide the care, with the negotiations effectively arbitrated by a third party organization made up of sickness funds and provider organizations. The government plays more of a regulatory role, outlining the basic conditions that should govern the delivery and availability of healthcare.

4.4 THE BELGIAN HEALTHCARE SYSTEM

The Belgian healthcare system features a compulsory national health insurance, which covers major risks for the entire population and minor risks for about 88% of the population.[113] According to van Kemenade, "virtually the whole population in Belgium is insured against sickness and disablement under a publicly organized and controlled but privately managed universal, compulsory, health insurance system."[114] The delivery of healthcare is private, based on independent medical practice, and free choice of a doctor. Changes have occurred recently from the formerly predominant fee-for-service payment system.

Responsibility for health insurance, hospital costs and drugs remains with the national government, although it is being increasingly delegated to the regional or to Dutch and French speaking communities. The supervision of the system is the responsibility of the National Institute for Sickness and Invalidity Insurance (INAMI), established in 1963, which answers to the Ministry of Social Security. All persons are required to subscribe to one of 129 sickness funds (HIAs) or "mutualité" of their choice, which are organized in six major groupings, with nearly half being Catholic with the remainder being socialist or liberal. The management and administration of the national insurance scheme is the responsibility of non-governmental private nonprofit sickness funds.

The HIAs (Health Insurance Association) originated as mutual aid societies associated with the labour movement. The HIAs were similar in many ways to credit unions in Canada, but rather than providing credit, the HIAs provided other social benefits. The HIAs originally were formed in the 19th century on a local level to provide replacement income for sickness or disability in return for regular contributions.[115] From there, some mutualités offered to reimburse members for physician fees or drug expenses. The levels for contributions and benefits were decided at general meetings of the membership.

The law governing the legal status of mutualitiés was established in 1894. It entrenched the non-commercial and nonprofit status of HIAs. Much like credit unions, the original mutualités were formed primarily along ideological lines. Also much like credit unions, the local mutual aid societies formed regional federations and then national alliances. The HIAs are the main third-party purchasers of healthcare in Belgium. These are six of them including the Christian (45%), Socialist (29%), Occupation (15%), Liberal, Neutral and Auxiliary.[116]

Other key legislation was passed in 1944 and 1945, making membership in a mutualité of their choice compulsory for all private employees and their dependents. In 1963 membership in a mutualité was made compulsory for the self-employed and their dependents, and in 1965 it was extended to all government employees.[117]

Competition between the mutualités and the auxiliary fund takes place on a largely non-price basis, involving supplementary services. This is due to the fact that members have the option of changing their public insurer every three months. This movement of patients has lead to an imbalance of members in terms of health and financial status. This in turn, has undermined the ability of mutualtiés to break even and led to the pooling of mutualités' surpluses and deficits by the National Institute of Health Insurance, with any overall shortfall covered by government subsidies. As a result of the lack of incentives for cost-control by mutualités that arose from this system, since 1995, a risk-based capitation formula has been in place as a partial basis for the funding of the sickness funds. This was part of the prospective budget provided to mutualités by the government, who were then responsible for some share of actual spending above the budgeted amount (25% in the year 2000).[118]

(a) Administration of Healthcare

The federal authorities in Belgium are part of an extensive regulatory system that governs the Belgium Healthcare System.[119] This system includes regional authorities as well as the mutualités and healthcare providers. The federal authorities determine the employers' and employees' insurance premiums as well as the amount of the public subsidy. The authorities influence both global budget decisions as well as hospital budget-setting and hospital capital investment. In addition the Ministry of Economic Affairs fixes pharmaceutical prices.

INAMI, a central institution in the Belgian healthcare system,[120] is under the supervision of the intermediary of government commissioners. INAMI controls the administrative and financial management of healthcare insurance and benefits, as well as maternity benefits. INAMI's main responsibilities are to (i) organize the conditions of access to health benefits which are covered by mandatory insurance – including price-setting and regulation, (ii) ensure that the parties involved adhere to the regulations, and (iii) organize the cooperation between the parties involved in the healthcare system, including the numerous councils, committees and colleges.

INAMI is managed by a general committee which has an equal number of representatives from the employers and independent workers, salaried workers and insurance companies. INAMI's General Council of the Healthcare Service determines the general political orientations of healthcare, and is charged with adhering to the global budget proposals emanating from the Insurance Committee. In terms of the voting structure of the General Council, those involved in financing insurance coverage (the employers, salaried workers, independent workers and government workers) have 3/4 of the total votes, while the insurance firms account for the remaining 1/4. The General Council also sends an annual report to the government concerning the implementation of health legislation throughout the country. Under the General Council is the Insurance Committee, which is the organization that reflects the concerns of the insurance firms and care dispensers, with an equal number of representatives from each on the committee. A key task is to make proposals to the General Committee and to assist in the annual global budget deliberations for health services.

A key committee in the Belgian healthcare system is the Medical Control Service. It is made up of insurance-organizations representatives (medical doctors) and representatives of organizations representing various care practitioners (doctors, dentists, pharmacists, clinics and nurses). The Medical Control Service oversees the medical aspects of healthcare insurance, insurance allowable benefits. In particular, it holds inspects doctors and including pharmacists from INAMI and counsels doctors from insurance firms who do not follow the insurance rules or the Committee's directions. Under the Medical Control Service is the Restraining Chambers, which has the power to withhold from mutual insurance firms, for a period of five days to one year, reimbursements claimed by care dispensers who didn't conform to legal and regulatory arrangements. In particular, care dispensers are to refrain from prescribing unnecessary examinations and treatments, which are recorded by the control committee.

(b) Financing

The system is almost evenly financed by payroll taxes – levied on employees (who contribute a percentage of their salary) and employers (55%) – and general tax revenues (45%).[121] According to Nonneman, the financing of healthcare by payroll taxes alters the political costs of raising additional revenues for healthcare.[122] Calls for increased healthcare spending must be met by higher taxes in the labour market, resulting in lower net wages, higher employer costs, and unemployment.[123] This is in contrast to systems where healthcare costs are financed out of general revenues, where the increased taxes may either not be noticed or if they are, are not worth lobbying against. That is, "in this mixed funding system, trade unions and employer's organizations share part of the responsibility to keep medical expenditure growth in check."[124]

For both the general scheme (for major and minor risks for salaried employees) and the self-employed scheme (for major risks), the contribution rates for health insurance are fixed by law at 3.55% of income for the employee and 3.80% for the employer. The rate for the self-employed is 3.20% of their income.[125] It is important to note that there is no fixed upper limit for contributions and they are unrelated to risk. For individuals not falling into these categories (for example, if they have never worked in the formal sector), their health needs are covered by Public Municipal Welfare Centres either through direct coverage of healthcare costs, or by paying the required premiums to register with a public insurer.[126]

Healthcare officials report that while at present, waiting lists are virtually nonexistent, the costs of meeting that standard have resulted in the overall budget for the year being exceeded by a modest amount. The expectation was that the next year's budget would then be increased to meet this new higher level; however, in the meantime physicians would have to wait for payments for work performed near the end of the year.

(c) Role of the Private Sector

There is a difference in medical-care coverage depending on occupation, with medical-care benefits limited to major risks for the self-employed, but very broad for wage and salary earners.[127] About 60% of all hospitals are nonprofit private institutions, with a further 5% belonging to HIAs. There is a small number of private hospitals.[128] No distinction in coverage is made between private and public hospitals. Hospital services are paid on the basis of a negotiated fee schedule for physician services.

In 1945, with the introduction of national compulsory health insurance, the former practice of local insurance funds negotiating fees with physicians and pharmacists was abandoned, with the health insurance funds restricting themselves to the determination of reimbursement amounts.[129] However, concern that unrestricted fees would lead to high personal contributions resulted in a return to fee negotiations with healthcare providers in 1963. After a brief labour dispute, physicians were finally prepared to collaborate.

The fee schedule is described in the *nomenclature*, which is a very detailed list of all health services qualifying for reimbursement. The list describes the medical services assigning it a unique code, which lists its official negotiated fee, including possible reimbursement conditions and reimbursement amounts.[130]

Physicians in Belgium, including GPs, dentists and specialists, are paid on a fee-for-service basis, with the official fees negotiated between the representatives of the medical profession and the sickness funds. The fees-for-service are paid by patients who must seek reimbursement from their mutualité. Patients in general must pay a coinsurance share of the bill. Patients are reimbursed for between 60% and 75% of the negotiated fee, with higher reimbursement rates existing for the poor and elderly (up to 90 or 100%). An important element of the Belgium healthcare market is the free choice of a doctor, which extends to specialists who do not need a referral from a GP.[131]

In terms of the market for compulsory health insurance, private-for-profit insurance companies are severely limited given the competitive advantage resulting from the nonprofit status of the HIAs. According to Nonneman and van Doorslaer, even the market for complementary insurance cannot be contested by the private sector, given the nonprofit tax exempt advantage held by the HIAs. In addition, the "economies of scale and scope give existing HIAs a 'first-mover advantage', which is difficult to offset even for the most efficient and large scale private operator."[132] Despite this disadvantage, some private for-profit companies in Belgium have recently emerged, providing voluntary health insurance as a supplement to the compulsory scheme.[133] Belgians use private insurance to cover both hospital costs and the costs of statutory co-payments; private insurance is offered by Belgian companies as a fringe benefit.[134]

(d) Hospital Sector

Global hospital capacity is controlled by the Ministry of Public Health, which gives accreditation to hospitals to operate a certain number of beds for each service category (including acute care, surgery and maternity). Accreditation is granted only if the proposed hospital, either new construction or alteration, respects national planning.[135] The accreditation criteria are developed at the national level, but are implemented by the respective communities. The requirements for accreditation relate to staffing, size of rooms, number of beds, etc., which are all required if reimbursement is to be obtained from the public system.

Table 4: Hospitals in Belgium – 1997 (selected statistics)

	Gen. Hospital	Psych. Hosp.	Total
–Number of Private Hospitals	152 (72%)	59 (28%)	211
–Number of Beds in Private Hospitals	34,000	12,814	46,814
–Admissions (thousands) – 1996	1,120	68	1,188
–Number of Public Hospitals	100 (90%)	12 (10%)	112
–Number of Beds in Public Hospitals	23,431	3,869	27,300
–Admissions (thousands) – 1996	749	22	771
–Total Number of Hospitals (% Private)	252 (60%)	71 (83%)	323
–Total Number of Beds (% Private)	57,433 (59%)	16,683 (77%)	74,116
–Total Admissions – 1996 (% Private)	1,869 (60%)	90 (75%)	1,959

Source: European Union of Independent Hospitals (2001).

Table 4 indicates the nature of the Belgian hospital network. As can be seen, the private sector is responsible for a slight majority of general hospitals and a clear majority of psychiatric hospitals. As of 1997, 60% of the general hospitals and 83% of psychiatric hospitals were private. In terms of general hospitals, the private sector provides approximately 60% of the beds and has 60% of all admissions. In terms of psychiatric hospitals, the private sector provides 77% of the beds and has 75% of all admissions.

Apart from control over hospital planning, the federal authorities plan the level of high technology equipment for the different areas of the country, with the plan being compulsory for the regional authorities.[136]

(e) Recent Developments

The Belgian system is seen as quite remarkable, given its absence of waiting lists. Belgian officials cite a number of reasons for the result. First, there historically was larger capacity built into the Belgian healthcare system, both in terms of hospital infrastructure, and in terms of the number of physicians, which has kept physician costs down. For example, during the period 1979-1994, general practitioners' incomes fell by 27% and specialists' incomes were reduced by 38%, causing some doctors to leave the profession.[137]

The share of the global healthcare budget paid by patients – either out of pocket or through private insurance – has increased over the years from 12% in 1987 to 17% in 1994.[138] This was the result of a royal decree in the early 1990's which increased the co-payments and coinsurance amounts for visits to a generalist from 20% to 30% and for specialist consultations from 25% to 40%. In 1994, co-payments and insurance were increased for clinical tests and medical imaging.[139] Some argue that this was done to reduce the expenditure on healthcare by raising the costs to patients.[140] However, given the effect on particular groups, a rebate – termed a social exemption – is provided to designated groups (widows, orphans, retired and disabled as well as minimum-wage recipients) for coinsurance and co-payments above a yearly total of BF 15 000. In addition, all households are eligible for a fiscal exemption – which is a deduction from income taxes – for co-payments and coinsurance payments above a certain threshold, which is determined by the household's gross taxable income.[141]

4.5 THE SWEDISH HEALTHCARE SYSTEM

The Swedish Healthcare system has three key features; (i) decentralized decision making by local public authorities, i.e., the (CC) county councils, (ii) exclusive territories (or monopoly service areas) for the delivery of health services by county councils and (iii) an integrating of financing and provision of health services by the county councils (that is, they own and operate their own facilities).[142] According to Saltman, healthcare services in Sweden are viewed as only one element of the welfare state and are considered a social good – with payment for the cost of these services viewed as a social responsibility, which is part of the cost of a decent society.[143]

Provinces used to be the main political units in Sweden. Today they are no longer of any significance and Sweden is divided into counties.[144] The county administrative boards look after the obligations of the government within the county, with the head of the county administrative board, the county governor appointed by the government. The councillors in the county council regions are elected directly by the county citizens, with the county councils/regions having the right to levy taxes. For the four levels of government in Sweden the governing bodies are as follows; at the national level there is parliament, at the regional level, the regional council assembly; at the county level, the county council assembly; and at the municipal level, the municipal council. Self-government in county councils and municipalities is one of the main principles of the organization of Swedish society.

There are 6 medical healthcare regions, which are divided up into 20 county councils and one local authority (Gotland) and are responsible for providing health services under the Health and Medical Services Act.[145] The population of the county council/region/municipal regions as of 1999 ranged from a high of 1.8 million for Stockholm County Council, to a low of 57 thousand for the Gotland Municipality, with an average population of 422 thousand.[146] The County Councils operate health services in a number of ways: there are 900 health centres offering Primary Care, 80 general hospitals at the County level, and 9 Regional hospitals.[147] There is a modest variation in the percent of rateable income levied by the County councils, with a high of 10.43 in Örebro county to a low of 9.13 in Jämtland, with an average imposition 9.79.[148]

The Federation of County Councils is the national organization that represents the councils in all policy matters. It is independent of the central government and finances its activities through member fees. On behalf of the county councils, it also negotiates with the personnel employed by the county council.

Independent of the County Council, are the municipalities at the local level, with population varying from 3,000 to 740,000. The municipalities are responsible for the delivery and financing of long term care for the elderly and the disabled, and for long-term psychiatric care. The municipalities have the power to levy their own taxes which are proportional to income.[149]

According to Saltman and von Otter, "the debate over appropriate levels and mechanisms of health sector accountability reflects two fundamental shifts in the underlying policy context."[150] The first is that the national government faces strong internal and external pressures to restrain overall public expenditures, particularly for healthcare. The second is the increased awareness among most Swedish policymakers of the limitations of traditional health planning models. According to Saltman and von Otter, this skepticism exists at both the national level with traditional command-and-control approaches to problem solving, and at the county level where operating decisions must be taken and defended. The existing approach has resulted in waiting periods of up to two years for certain elective surgical procedures.[151]

In terms of overall Swedish health expenditures, as a percentage of GDP, there was a remarkable reduction over the 5 year period 1992-1997; a 40% reduction in beds, a 20% reduction in staff, and an 8% reduction in costs. The drop has been attributed to a shift in the responsibility of nursing homes and other elderly care residential services from the 26 county councils to the 284 municipalities. The shift removed 0.9% from the reported cost of the Swedish health system.[152]

The role of the central government in Sweden regarding health services is set forth in the Health and Medical Services Act (1982). The Act assures the entire population good health and care on equal terms, and guarantees that every county council will offer good health and medical services to persons living within its boundaries and with also promote their health.[153] In addition, the National Board of Health and Welfare is the advisory and supervisory agency for health and social services, overseeing the county councils. It has the responsibility to ensure that the health and social services provided by the county councils meet the goals established by the central government.[154]

In Sweden, patients have the right to choose among primary healthcare providers, including the option to use either the local primary healthcare centre or hospital outpatient departments. The country councils however influence this decision; charging a lower fee if a primary care centre is chosen (between SEK 60 and SEK 160) than outpatient care at a hospital is selected (between SEK 150 and SEK 200).[155]

(a) Financing

The cost of health services amounted to SEK 128 billion in 1996, or 7.6% of GNP. This includes the costs for pharmaceutical preparations and dental care. About 90% of this sum was spent on care provided or financed by the county councils.[156]

Healthcare services account for about 85% of the operations of the county councils. As of 1997, most of the operations were financed by tax revenues (77%) with 9% coming from central government subsidies and reimbursements and the remaining 4% from individual payments.[157] The county councils have the power to levy a proportional tax on the incomes of residents which amounted to an average rate of 9.79% in 1999.[158] For other than care funded from individual payments, the costs of healthcare are paid directly by the county councils.

Nominal fees are charged patients for services; however, the national parliament has set a ceiling on the total amount of direct patient fees that can be paid over a 12-month period, a maximum SEK 900, not including inpatient care. There is some variation in these fees within the county councils, for example the fee for consulting a physician in a primary health centre ranges from SEK 100 to SEK 150, while the fee for consulting a specialist at a hospital ranges from SEK 150 to SEK 250.[159] For inpatient care, the normal fee is SEK 80 per day, with reductions for pensioners and low income groups. No fee is charged for children under the age of 18[160] or for those who suffer from chronic disease.[161]

It is important to note that the public share of total health expenditure in Sweden has fallen over time, from 92.5% in 1980 to 83.8% in 1998.[162]

(b) Role of the Private Sector

It has been argued that in Sweden, a common goal of governments in the post-1945 period, was to provide healthcare of a quality high enough to satisfy all segments of the population, thereby reducing the demand for private alternatives.[163] According to Garpenby (1995:696) there had been no real demand for private health insurance until the 1980's. After that, due to the waiting time for certain medical procedures within the public system, a Swedish insurance company, Skandia, began to offer private health insurance.[164] Of the approximately 120,000 who are privately insured, in 90% of the cases, the employer pays the fees in order to reduce employees' long term sick leave.[165] Those insured are guaranteed immediate access, but the insurance does not cover acute care. Since 1988, Swedish law has prohibited the deduction of private insurance premiums from income taxes.[166]

In terms of employees in the public health services, there were 23,000 doctors, 70,000 nurses, 64,000 auxiliary nurses, 5,000 physiotherapists and 4,000 occupational therapists as of 1997.[167] In contrast to Canada, the majority of doctors in Sweden are salaried, with the average salary of a hospital doctor with specialist qualification at 38,000 SEK per month. In Sweden there is a shortage of nurses with specialist training and it is also difficult to recruit doctors to certain geographic areas and to certain specialist fields.[168] In addition to public medical staff, there are some 1,700 physicians and 2,200 physiotherapists working in private practices. They are paid by county councils on a fee-for-service basis (per visit/call) in accordance with a fee scale determined by the central government.[169] As of 1997, 7% of registered general practitioners in Sweden worked as private practitioners, mainly in large cities.[170] The limited number of medical staff working in private practice has been affected somewhat by the emphasis on the relatively large proportion of medical services provided in hospitals. The number of general practitioners as a percentage of the total number of doctors is low (20%). There are also low numbers of visits per person and year to primary care doctors.

While the county councils cannot directly control the establishment of doctors in private practice, they have indirect control by controlling the public financing of private practitioners.[171]

The primary healthcare sector in Sweden plays a Gatekeeper role, with referrals made to specialists either at the county or regional level when needed. While primary care is mainly publicly provided, some primary care is privately provided. In fact in 2000, 25% of all physician consultations in outpatient care were conducted at private facilities which are relatively common in large cities. They are private in the sense they are privately run, with a majority of them having contracts with the county councils which in turn reimburse patients for their costs. To be publicly funded, an agreement with the county council is required. Such agreements stipulate that private entrepreneur must work full-time in private practice.[172]

Private inpatient care, consists mainly of nursing homes, geriatric care and psychiatric care. As of 2001, there were around 200 nursing homes privately owned and operated.[173]

(c) Recent Reforms

Sweden experimented with a variety of reforms in the 1990s.[174] Harrison and Calltorp (2000:236) conclude that "despite their fashion-like development, Sweden's competitive reforms appear to have had lasting consequences for its health system. The reforms gave patients more ability to exercise choice over health services and enhance the responsiveness of health providers and county councils to patient concerns."

The reforms in the 1990's included (i) the *Patient Choice and Care Guarantee*, (ii) the *Family Doctor System* (iii) the *Purchaser-provider split* and (iv) *Competing Policy Agendas*. The *Patient Choice and Care Guarantee* was designed to have the money follow the patient, in the sense of providing choice as to where to obtain elective care, rather than assigning patients to hospitals on the basis of residence. If an individual chose to have care outside his local area, the local hospital or county council would have to pay the providing hospital for the patient's care. In addition to this obligation, the guarantee of treatment within three months for certain therapies and the right to seek treatment elsewhere, required the Central government to grant extra funding to the cc's (Harrison and Calltorp (2000:223).

According to Harrison and Calltorp, the reforms of the 1990s ushered in a new phase of market reforms. The new initiatives involve (i) competition among private and semi-private providers, (ii) renewed efforts to transform hospitals into publicly-owned companies and privatize their services in a number of counties, and (iii) a gradual increase in the number of physicians who entirely or partly own their own medical facilities and contract with the public system to provide ambulatory services.[175] Harrison and Calltorp conclude that "Sweden's market-oriented reforms do promise to help keep the public health system flexible and responsive to the needs and concerns of its citizens."[176] The available evidence, they argue, indicates that the market-oriented reforms resulted in improvements in hospital productivity and efficiency with no adverse effect on the quality of overall healthcare.[177]

Diderichsen (1999:2) argues that the central government cost-control policies, including a cutting of grants to the county councils and legislation preventing increases in local taxation rates – coupled with a reduction in local tax revenues due to unemployment – have resulted in a decreased access to care. A number of responses have occurred, with some counties opting for increased private provision, and increasing numbers of medical staff leaving for the private sector. The result is that more than 20% of hospital beds are now privately financed.[178]

Several county councils have established separate purchasing organizations: as of 1994, 14 out of 26 county councils had done so. For healthcare, the contracts are usually based on DRG's for case payments, complemented with price or volume restrictions and quality guarantees.[179] With respect to hospital-based outpatient care, weighted visits are used as the per case payment scheme, with per diem payments sometimes included.

Overall, substantial variation exists in the contracting out of services between the county councils. Contracting out more is common for elderly and primary care, although recently some discussion has taken place regarding the contracting out of inpatient care.[180]

(d) Stockholm County Council

Stockholm County Council, the largest County Council in Sweden, has a record of experimentation with alternative approaches to healthcare delivery. Stockholm County has 1.8 million inhabitants, and covers an area of about 6,500 km2 with a distance of 180 km from north to south. Within the Stockholm County Council are 26 municipalities of varying sizes ranging from the City of Stockholm to rural, sparsely-populated municipalities. The region is an archipelago with 24,000 islands of which 150 are inhabited.[181]

Stockholm County Council has recently agreed to extend its agreement with St. Göran's Hospital and Capio AB, the owner of the hospital, by 4 years to the end of 2006.[182] St. Göran's hospital is the first emergency hospital in Sweden with a private owner. With 1,500 employees, 240 beds and a turnover over SEK 800 million in 1999, St. Göran's has clinics for emergency care, orthopaedics, medicine, surgery, anaesthesia, x-rays, physiology and in-house service organization. Capio reports that as of the year 2000, the price that the Stockholm County Council was paying St. Göran's is between 7 and 12 percent lower than the prices at other hospitals within Stockholm County Council.

The owner, Capio AB, provides healthcare services in thirty medical specialist areas. Capio, formed in 1994, is currently operating in Sweden, Norway, Denmark, the UK, Switzerland and Poland, and is listed on the Stockholm Stock Exchange. Capio states that "instead of traditional competition, Capio has chosen to collaborate with public healthcare. Furthermore, "Capio's ambition is to be the healthcare provider that in the best possible way fulfils the demands from both patients, the public healthcare as well as from companies and organizations."

Capio's clients are primarily county councils and municipalities, as well as companies purchasing occupational and healthcare services. Its care units have agreements with public sector principles, in which patients can obtain care on the same terms as within the public healthcare system, with the same patient fees and waiting list regulations in force. In particular all patients are welcome and patient fees are the same as in the public healthcare system.

The Stockholm County Council is currently planning to implement procurement of emergency healthcare services. As a start, the scope of the procurement is a contract period of five years with the option of a two-year extension, at a planned cost of ten billion Swedish kronor per year. According to Stockholm County Council officials, the procurement can benefit from the experience gained by the procurement undertaken by the Simrishamn hospital in southern Sweden.[183]

Procurement is being pursued "because the politicians wish to increase the diversity of suppliers. They also want to see new solutions to the ways in which healthcare is conducted. With increased diversity and several different suppliers, they want to create competition that stimulates progress in healthcare."[184]

4.6 THE AUSTRALIAN HEALTHCARE SYSTEM*

Australia has a population of approximately 19 million who live in a country consisting of a federation of six states and two territories. The population is unevenly distributed, with roughly two-thirds living in the ten largest cities, and the remainder spread over a very large geographic area. There exists in Australia a well-organized healthcare system with universal access to needed healthcare irrespective of ability to pay, a strong private healthcare sector and a medical profession that is politically influential.

(a) The History of Australian Healthcare system

In order to understand how and why the Australian healthcare system is funded and operates in the way it does, a little background information is valuable. Until the 1930's healthcare financing essentially included the wealthy paying their own way, Friendly Societies and lodges insuring the middle classes, and the poor receiving charitable services. Public healthcare services that were seen to benefit all of society were provided by the state (Lewis 2001).

The National Health Services Act of 1948-49 provided for medical practitioners to continue on a fee-for-service basis with half of the fee to be paid by the Federal Government and only remote areas to have a salaried service. The (Australian) British Medical Association rejected this scheme, as they were very wary of the Federal Government as pay master. The continued strength of the medical association and their apparent desire for control of the healthcare system has had

---

* This section was written by Marian Shanahan

considerable impact on subsequent policy decisions in the healthcare sector in Australia.

Some key events in the history of the healthcare system in Australia are:

- 1974 – Introduction of a tax-funded universal heath insurance scheme called Medibank. This scheme was administered by the Health Insurance Commission and was responsible for the payment of fees to medical practitioners and state hospitals (Gardner 1997).

- 1975-1981 – Medibank was gradually dismantled with a return to voluntary insurance with Federal rebates available only to those in registered funds and an end to free hospital care.

- 1984 – Medicare was introduced. It was funded through the tax system including a levy on taxable income. Medibank provided free inpatient and outpatient public hospital care and public funding of 85% of medical fees.

- 1990s – A two-tier health insurance system was promoted with the provision of public subsidies for private insurance companies.

- 1999 – The Federal Government introduced a 30% rebate on the cost of private health insurance.

- 2000 – The Federal Parliament passed a change in insurance legislation to permit Life Time health insurance, with differential premiums.

(b) Overview of Australian Healthcare system

A basic tenet of the Australian Healthcare system is universal access to needed healthcare irrespective of ability to pay. Medicare, a national scheme, is paid from general taxation. A 1% levy on taxable income covers ambulatory medical services, and provides for all residents to get treatment in public hospitals without charge. Other available benefits include cash benefit programs for pharmaceuticals and subsidies for nursing home care.

A dominant feature of the Australian political system is the division of powers between Federal and State governments with the responsibilities for health services shared by both (Hall, 1999). The Federal Government

Table 5: Key indicators

Key indicators	1997/98
Total health services expenditure (million – Aus Dollars)	$ 47,030
Total Expenditure as a % of GDP	8.3 %
Health expenditure as average of total State outlays	19 %
Health expenditure of total Federal Government outlays	14 %
Health services expenditure per capita (Aus Dollars)	$ 2,523

Source AIHW 2000

is directly responsible for the financing of medical services, pharmaceutical benefits, and aged care residential services whereas the state governments, with some Federal Government financial assistance, are responsible for the funding and operation of the public hospital services, mental health services, community support programs, and women's and children's services. Five-year Medicare agreements between the Federal Government and the States provide the basis for the funding for the period of the agreement. For some components of the healthcare system, the Federal Government provides funds outside of the Medicare agreement, which the State governments may supplement with their own funding. Examples of these are National Youth Suicide Strategy, National Mental Health Strategy, women's health, AIDs, family planning, drug strategies, health services for the homeless, child immunization, and health education and practice.

There also exists a private health insurance system which operates alongside the universal system. Private health insurance covers treatment either in a private or public hospital, for that which is not covered under Medicare – primarily accommodation costs in private hospitals but also a number of ancillary services. In 1997/98, the public system accounted for 68.6% (Federal Government 45.2% and the State and local governments 23.4%) of total healthcare expenditures, with the non-government sector accounting for 31.1% (AIHW 2000). Historically, the control of global budgets and ability to negotiate fees by the State and Federal governments have ensured that the rate of growth in expenditures has been relatively stable. However, the split in responsibilities for the healthcare systems between the State and Federal governments, further compounded with the existence of a private health insurance industry, means that it is difficult to significantly revamp the existing system.

At 8.3% of total GDP, the proportion spent on health may be less than in some other countries. Yet there is considerable debate in Australia over what the appropriate amount and mix of healthcare expenditures should be. Some areas of continued controversy include whether an increase in medical fees would affect the amount and quality of healthcare offered, the need for increased funding for public hospitals to decrease waiting lists for surgery, whether there are sufficient resources allocated to care for the elderly, the lack of healthcare service for those in rural areas, and rising expenditures on pharmaceuticals and new technologies.

(c) Medical Services

All Australians are insured for medical services provided outside hospitals by private practitioners on a fee-for-service basis, at 85% of the fee set under the Medicare Benefits Schedule (MBS). The out-of-pocket expense, between the scheduled fee and the 85% rebate, is referred to as the gap. The gap is subject to an indexed maximum for any individual service and to a safety net limit per year for a family group. However, doctors are free to set their own fees above the MBS fee, in which case the excess must be borne by the patient. Doctors who send their bills in bulk accept the 85% MBS as full payment, avoiding bad debts, and lowering administration costs. Patients who visit these doctors bear no out-of-pocket costs for their visit. In 1995/96, 71% of medical services were bulk billed. Co-payment by the private health insurance funds on medical services are not allowed; that is, they are not allowed to cover medical payments over and above the schedule fee. Recently though, legislation has been passed to allow contractual arrangements between doctors providing services in private facilities and insurers to pay fees higher than those scheduled.

The Federal Government sets the MBS fees. Because these fees are the subject of ongoing discussion and negotiation with the Australian Medical Association, as with any union, the AMA expresses continual dissatisfaction with many of the fees under the MBS. While the fees are set, there is no cap on the total payment to GPs. In other words, there is no limiting of the total number of visits to GPs that may be billed to the MBS.

Medical services in public hospitals are free for public patients. Medicare provides a 75% rebate for medical services for private patients in both public and private hospitals. Private insurance covers the other 25% of the MBS fee for private patients, but as described above, co-payments for fees over and above scheduled payments are not permitted unless the doctor and the insurers have negotiated a contractual arrangement. This recent change occurred as a result of many patients receiving treatment in private hospitals and having to pay fees that were often higher than their annual private health insurance premiums.

(d) Hospitals

Under the Medicare Agreement all Australians are entitled to free access to public hospital accommodation and medical treatment. The flow of funds from the Federal Government to the states and territories for public hospitals takes place through specific purpose grants, and is based primarily on a population formula. There is also a fiscal equalization formula which results in the wealthier states transferring monies to the less rich states. In 1997/98, 58.6% of State and Territory Government total health expenditures were for the operating costs of public hospitals.

Hospitals in Australia are referred to as either private or public, with the nomenclature of "public" usually referring to the proprietorship of a hospital where the board of directors being appointed by the Minister of Health. There are exceptions to this, with some religiously-based hospitals functioning as public hospitals and some privately owned hospitals having agreements with their State government to provide care to public patients. The situation is further complicated by the fact that many public hospitals provide care to private patients.

Payment for hospital activity usually takes place via one of the following methods: historical based funding; per diem (usually for non-acute care and nursing homes); or case mix funding (Duckett, p118). Each state or territory determines the allocation method to hospitals in their jurisdiction. Medicare has eliminated financial barriers to accessing public hospitals care but waiting lists are now seen as one method of managing excess demand for hospital care. Access to public hospitals is determined by whether the patient will be harmed by a delay in admission to hospital. Admission to the hospital may be by direct admission through the emergency department or by a doctor who has admitting privileges to the hospital, usually a specialist in non-rural areas.

Private hospitals, which increasingly tend to be owned by corporate hospital chains, are regulated by the state – with the number of beds and licences being tradable commodities (Duckett 2000). Private hospitals range from small facilities providing limited services to a few large hospitals providing a multitude of specialist services but most do not have emergency departments.

As is the situation in most developed countries, there has been a decline in hospital beds per capita over the last 20 years, with an accompanying increase in separations from hospital. This is as a result of shorter lengths of stay due to changes in technology, procedures, and pharmaceuticals. In Australia, despite a decline in the number of people covered by health insurance since the early 1980s there has been an increase of 77% of separations from private hospitals with only 30% in public hospitals (Duckett, 2000).

(e) Pharmaceuticals

Australia has a national pharmaceutical benefit scheme (PBS) that subsidizes the cost of listed, prescribed medications dispensed by private retail pharmacies. Over 90% of the drugs available for prescription by doctors are listed on the schedule (Mooney,1999). The PBS is a co-payment scheme, subject to annual ceilings. Patients categorized as concessional beneficiaries (pensioners and persons in low income groups with a healthcare card) are charged a co-payment per PBS item of $3.30 up to a total expenditure of $171.60 per year, after which no co-payment is required. General beneficiaries pay a co-payment of $20.60 per PBS item until they pay $631.20 in a year, after which they would only pay $3.30 per item (AIHW, 2000). If a PBS item is priced above benchmark price by the private pharmacy, the patient may pay more than the co-payment, and this is not included in the safety net.

Application for a drug to be listed on the PBS requires a submission to the Pharmaceutical Benefits Advisory Committee. The submission needs to demonstrate that the drug is effective, and cost effective. As part of the listing process, the government establishes a price for the drug based on recommendations by the PBAC. Despite the government's monopsonistic power, expenditures on pharmaceuticals is increasing by about 20% annually. In 1997/98, total expenditure on non-hospital pharmaceuticals was $5335 million, with 59% paid by public-sector benefits (either PBS or Veteran's Affairs).

Prior to listing on the PBS, a submission, which demonstrates the drug's safety, effectiveness, and cost-effectiveness analyses, must be made to the Pharmaceutical Benefits Advisory Committee. This committee, which is comprised of experts, recommends to the Federal Government whether a drug should be listed on the PBS.

(f) Aged Care

Care for the aged and the disabled can be provided in the client's home or in residential care settings. The provision of residential care services is the responsibility of the state government or privately owned nursing homes, but the funding of these services is the responsibility of Federal Government (assisted by residents' co-payments). The amount of the Federal Government's subsidy varies with the resident's level of dependency and need for care. Admission to residential care facilities is conditional on an aged care assessment that determines whether or not an individual could be maintained in his home with additional home support.

The majority of elderly live at home, with care provided by family. Support programs are offered under the umbrella organization Home and Community Care (HACC), which aims to provide an integrated package of non-institutional care in the home. Services include home nursing, respite care, food services, aged daycare, and transport services. The State and Federal governments administer HACC and both levels of governments share costs.

With the challenges of an aging population, a number of changes in legislation and funding have occurred in recent years. Legislation passed in 1997, removed any distinction between nursing and hostel facilities, meaning that all providers would receive equal levels of funding for residents with similar needs. The residential component of funding for residential care consists of a basic daily care charge and a contribution to capital costs of the facility, and depends upon the resident's income (for daily charges) and assets (for capital related payments) (Duckett, 2000).

As is the trend elsewhere, funding for aged care is shifting towards community based care. From 1985 to 1997, the proportion of all funding going towards nursing homes declined form 80 to 63%, while expenditure on hostels increased from just under 5% to 13% and community care increased from 15 to 21% (Howe, 1999)

(g) Private Health Insurance

As discussed previously, the private health insurance industry plays a major role in the Australian Healthcare system. Private health insurance covers treatment for private patients, either in a private or public hospital. It provides for that which is not covered under Medicare, primarily accommodation costs in private hospitals but also a number of ancillary services. Unlike in the US, insurance premiums are most often paid by the individual, not by their employer.

The private health insurance industry, in Australia, has long been heavily regulated in terms of the types of products that may be offered, the prices charged and the risk-sharing arrangements. To ensure that private health insurance is affordable, community rating has been required since 1953 (Hall, 1999). Despite this, the number of Australians with private health insurance fell from 50.2% in 1984 to 30.5% in 1998 (AIHW 2000). Reasons for this decline include the rise in insurance premiums (on average, 9.8% per year from 1989/90 to 1995/96); the unpredictability of out-of-pocket expenses; and the fact that two patients could receive the same treatment, in the same hospital, by the same doctor and one might receive a large bill that is not reimbursable by insurance while the other does not pay anything (Hall, 1999).

In order to arrest the decline in the population holding private health insurance, the Federal Government introduced a number of initiatives including 'front end deductible' in late 1980s, exclusionary and exclusionary tables to permit exclusion of certain types of treatment; a 1% levy on all households with an income greater than $100,000 per annum who did not have private health insurance; and a 30% rebate on private health insurance premiums in 1999. This latter scheme meant that the Federal Government paid a direct subsidy to the contributor either directly once a private health insurance policy was purchased or through the taxation system. These recent changes have seen an initial increase from 30% to a high of 45.7% of the population having private health insurance.

Private health insurance covers accommodation costs of private patients, benefits equal to 25% of the gap between Medicare benefits and scheduled fees for private medical services in hospitals, and a wide range of ancillary services. Current legislation prevents the payment of the total gap between Medicare benefits and scheduled fees; however, as discussed earlier, there are now some options which allow coverage of an agreed gap between what the practitioner charges and what Medicare pays (PHI).

In addition to the 30% rebate, the Federal Government introduced changes to allow for Lifetime Cover to replace a strict community rating system. This change allows health funds to offer lifetime rates which offer lower premiums if an individual joins at a younger age.

(h) Access to care

While the financial burden of basic healthcare has been removed through the universal Medicare system, there remain several barriers to access. For example, as medical doctors have the right to practice where they desire, and to determine whether they will bulk bill, there is a shortage of both specialists and GPs in many rural areas. This often creates an inequitable distribution of healthcare services for rural residents. Not only do they not have local access to specialists as most are based in urban areas, but fewer GPs in rural areas choose to bulk bill. Thus the individual is faced with paying the whole fee, and submitting a claim for the rebate. And, as discussed previously, there are waiting lists in public hospitals for many types of surgeries, but waiting lists do not exist in private hospitals. But the additional financial burden of health insurance, plus gap fees and possibly fees beyond the gap may be beyond the financial means of a significant portion of the population.

While neither of these issues is unique to the Australian healthcare system, the complex division of powers between Federal and State governments makes many of the problems of the healthcare system difficult to address as they require the agreement of nine different Ministers of Health.

4.7 VIEWS OF THE MARKET ORIENTED REFORMS IN THE OECD

The impetus for an increased role for the private sector is often the result of perceived shortcomings with the public system. For example, Whitehead et al. (1997) argue that experiments with market-style reforms in Sweden can be attributed to the increase in waiting lists for elective surgery and reduced access to primary care among younger people. The British NHS reforms were influential in Sweden, where they were seen as a possible solution to the dilemma of controlling costs while maintaining a high level of public health services. Both the Social

Democrats and the Conservative-Liberal governments in the late 1980's and early 1990's saw market reforms as a making the public system more efficient.[185] However, the reforms led to a reallocation of resources between CC's and affected both hospital budgets and physician incomes; doctors then moved to resist developments that threatened them. To summarize one view, "the electorate and politicians across the political spectrum began to withdraw their support for market-type experiments and neo-conservative ideologies, once it became clear that exposure to market forces could weaken Sweden's social welfare system, reduce public employment and the threaten the country's historic commitment to social equality."[186]

In Australia, there is the view that private health initiatives do not alleviate the pressures on Australia's public hospitals – casualty waiting times, access to intensive care and elective surgery waiting lists. The reason, Davoren (2001) argues, is that much of the work of public hospitals in Australia involves looking after the chronically ill – as a result of chronic heart and lung disease, cancer, and stroke.[187] This group is less likely to be able to afford private insurance. Davoren (2001) also argues that premium rebates for purchasers of private insurance would be better spent in expanding public hospital capacity and addressing the shortage of specialist staff and appropriate support staff.[188]

In the U.K., there is considerable debate about the nature and direction of the recent market-oriented reforms. For example, Doyle and Bull (2000) argue that "collaboration between the public and private healthcare sectors, where it is sensible to do so, would serve the country better than continued isolation."[189] They point out that the case mix in private healthcare has shifted from simple elective surgery to include complex surgery such as coronary bypass, acute and subacute care, intensive care and cancer. Certain parts of the population, they argue, would be expected to pay more for guaranteed access, according to income, and those who could not afford to pay would have similar access funded by the state. They conclude that voters appreciate the goal of the NHS which is to pursue maximum gains within a limited budget in the abstract, and that it does not always work in any given individual case. In response, Keen (2000) argues that there are three policies that critical in deciding how to set out a framework for thinking about the relation between the NHS and private care.[190] First, he asks whether people in the UK would be comfortable with the present arrangements whereby people using private services can access them more quickly than NHS patients if they make supplementary contributions. Second, whether the private sector should undertake more elective surgery as recommended by Doyle and Bull, given that with a limited number of surgeons, the increased private activity would affect access to NHS elective and emergency services. Keen suggests the real question is whether UK society wants both the private and public systems to be larger. Third, Keen suggests that a mixed system implies a change in the objective of the health system from a principle that healthcare should be available to all regardless of income or where people live (the current NHS equity principle) to an objective that the system should promote consumer choice and a role for the NHS as a safety net for people unable to take out insurance.

Reforms to the German healthcare system have been prompted by the fact that the German economy has been in recession twice in the past two years with an unemployment rate of 10%. Germany, like France and Italy, "suffers from a killer combination of an aging population, low birth rates and generous pension provision."[191] The public health system in Germany had a deficit of 2.8 billion Euro in 2001 and an expected deficit of 2.5 billion in 2002 with insurers reporting big losses.[192] The reforms have included cuts to what have been seen as the more outlandish features of the German system, including lifestyle drugs and well as taxi fares to doctor's appointments.[193] To bring healthcare spending back under control, the government is proposing measures to reduce the public health service's annual cost, and in particular to reduce the contributions back to 13% from the current rate of 14.4%.[194] On October 9, 2003 the Rürup commission submitted a 377 page report proposing a flat-rate payment of €210 (US $244) a month on all taxpayers irrespective of income, to be extended to groups currently exempt (civil servants and the unemployed).[195] While all sides acknowledge the need for reform, it has been argued that the German consensus system of politics has stymied any attempt to push through the needed reforms.[196] Regarding future prospects, Altenstetter (2003) predicts that co-payments will remain an essential element of the German system, and that the issue of the German health system's dependence on payroll taxes will continue to be at the heart of any debate.[197]

Recent reforms have addressed three ongoing problems facing the French healthcare system, but as yet they remain unsolved. According to Rodwin (2003), the problems are 1) a striking disparity in the geographic distribution of health resources; 2) a newly perceived problem of uneven quality in the distribution of health services; and 3) within Europe, France is still among the higher spenders.[198] Despite these current shortcomings, efforts are being made to address them. Rodwin concludes that the French healthcare system provides a number of lessons for other countries. First, it is possible to achieve universal coverage without a "single payer" system. Second, regarding lessons for the U.S. system, he argues that universal coverage can be achieved in a gradual fashion. Third, the French system also demonstrates that universal coverage can be achieved without excluding private insurers from the supplementary insurance market. As evidence, he points to the thriving nonprofit insurance sector (*mutuelles*) as well as commercial companies.[199]

One view of the reforms to the Belgian healthcare system is provided by Schokkaert and Van de Voorde (2003). Changes to include a risk adjustment system of reimbursement to partially finance the Belgian sickness funds have, they argue, not been accompanied with the necessary instruments for the funds to exert a real influence on expenditures. Schokkaert and Van de Voorde (2003) identify a development toward fiercer competition in the supplementary market and argue that "cream skimming" in the compulsory market is likely to increase. They argue that competition between sickness funds is likely to take place through the quality of their services, which will increase costs. They conclude that it is "advisable to strengthen gradually the regulatory role played by the sickness funds. This requires that policy makers start thinking about what instruments for cost containment could be given to the individual sickness funds."[200]

4.8 SUMMARY OF THE SELECTED HEALTHCARE SYSTEMS

Table 6 summarizes a number of these characteristics, while Table 1 provides some statistical measures related to the output of these systems. As emphasized by the OECD when it distributes its data base, statistical measures comparing health systems should be used with caution. It was felt important, nonetheless, to report a number of measures from the most often cited source – the OECD – in order to provide some context to the discussion.

In the next section, a number of issues related to the operation and performance of the healthcare systems discussed in this paper will be examined. In some cases, the issues that arise can be traced to the type of system in place, either Social Welfare or Social Insurance based. In others, they are related to the variety of ways in which these systems operate in the respective countries.

Table 6: Characteristics of the Healthcare Systems in selected OECD Countries

System	Australia	Belgium	Canada	France	Germany	Sweden	UK
I. Public Health Services Coverage							
A. Basic Services							
– Free			√				
– Co-payment	√	√		√	√	√	√
B. Coverage							
– Voluntary							
– Opting Out of Public					√		
– Compulsory	√	√	√	√	√	√	√
C. Extended Coverage							
– Public Premium		√			√		
– Private Premium	√	√	√	√	√	√	√
D. Nature of Access to Physician							
– Free Choice of Physician	√[7]	√	√	√	√	√	√[5]
– Limited	√[7]						
E. Nature of Access to Specialist							
– Direct (non-emergency)		√		√	√		
– Referral from GP (non-emergency)	√		√			√	√
II. Compensation							
A. Physician Services							
– Fee for Service (predominantly)		√	√	√	√		
– Salary (predominantly)						√	√
– Combination (includes capitation)	√						
B. Physician Fee Determination							
– Negotiated with Government	√		√			√	√
– Negotiated with Insurer		√		√	√		
– Market Determined (extra billing)	√						

System	Australia	Belgium	Canada	France	Germany	Sweden	UK
C. Hospital Services							
– Free	√		√				
– Co-payment		√		√	√	√	√
III. Financing							
– General Taxation	√		√			√	√
– Joint Premiums Employee/Employer		√		√	√		
IV. Administration							
– Local							
– Regional	√³	√⁴	√	√	√	√	
– National	√³	√⁴					√
V. Private Health Services							
A. Private Insurance							
– Basic Services (some groups)	√				√		√
– Extended Coverage	√	√	√	√	√	√	√
B. Private Hospitals							
(i) Entry Conditions							
– Entry Prohibited			√			√²	
– Restricted Entry	√	√		√	√		√
(ii) Revenue Sources							
– Contracts with Public System				√		√²	√
– Private Insurance	√			√	√		√
C. Hospital Charges							
– Negotiated or Regulated	√	√⁶		√	√	√²	√
– Non-regulated							

Notes:
1. Group 2 coverage allows free choice of doctor and direct access to specialist care (nominal fee).
2. Hospital trial
3. Shared Responsibility
4. Increasingly delegated to the regional level.
5. Restricted within a geographic area
6. Does not include "amenity services" not covered by Social Security.
7. Participants in public hospitals have limited choice of physician otherwise free choice of physician.

CHAPTER V

ISSUES IN THE OPERATION AND PERFORMANCE OF THE SELECTED OECD COUNTRIES

Given the healthcare systems reviewed, this section provides an analysis of the differences in their operation and performance. It is useful to break down the analysis into four broad categories: issues related to the allocation system, issues related to the insurance function, issues related to competition between healthcare providers and issues related to the total funding of the system.

5.1 ISSUES RELATED TO THE ALLOCATION SYSTEM

It is well known that there are different allocation systems that may be used to provide goods or services in an economy. For example, the allocation can be by willingness to pay, first-come-first-serve, or based on merit. Often issues related to the operation and performance of healthcare systems are related to the differences in these allocation systems.

(a) Allocation by Willingness to Pay

In non-healthcare markets, consumer sovereignty is said to prevail. That is, private-sector firms compete to meet the desires of the consumer for goods or services. In private markets, the full-information competitive outcome results in an allocation of goods based on willingness to pay.

Given the demand for the good (which is the horizontal summation of individual demands) and the supply conditions governing the production of the service, the competitive price and quantity price and results in care being allocated to those individuals who place a value on the care which is greater that the price prevailing in the market. While often related to income, this willingness to pay for care by individuals is determined by individual preferences as well as the prices of other goods, either substitutes or complements.

A number of issues related to the allocation of healthcare resources can be illustrated with the aid of a simple model of the demand and supply

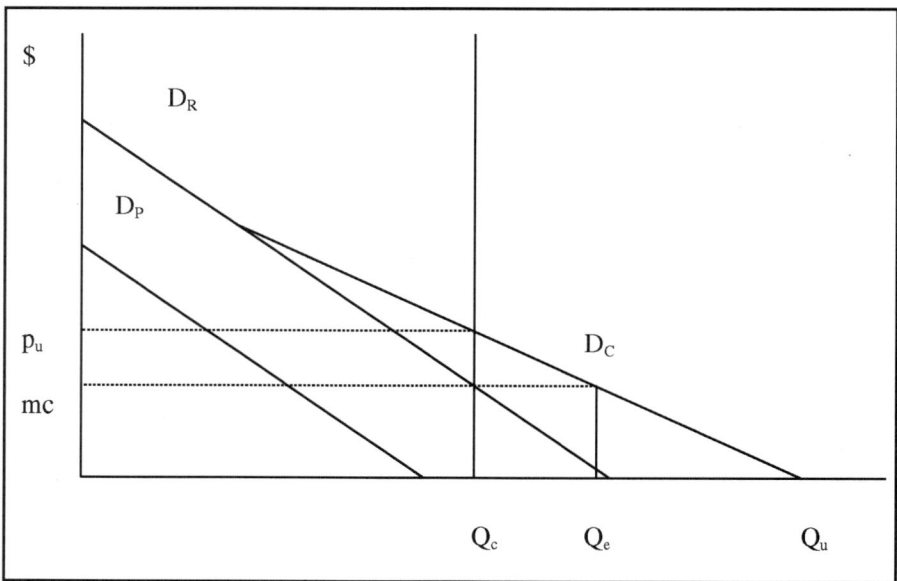

Figure 4: Demand and Supply for a Medical Procedure

of a particular medical procedure or operation. Figure 4 represents the demand for the medical procedure by two groups, R and P. The demand by group P is the line represented by D_p while the demand by group R is given by D_R. If we combine the demands by group R and group P, by summing horizontally, we get the combined total demand for operations per month which is given by the kinked line, D_C.

The horizontal line is the marginal cost of an operation, which is assumed for simplicity to be constant. This cost refers to an operation of quality level q_o.[201] In terms of supply, consider a public healthcare system which has chosen to allocate a total budget B for the particular medical procedure. This results in a particular capacity or number of procedures that can be provided, which is given by the vertical line Q_c. This capacity can be reflected as a total budget (B) divided by the average cost of the medical procedure (AC) or $Q_c = B/AC$.

There are a number of implications that emerge from the above analysis. First, suppose that marginal cost pricing is used. In that case, there would be an excess demand for operations for the month given by the distance Q_e-Q_c. A number of possible responses can be considered. First, capacity could be increased by the amount Q_e-Q_c which would eliminate the excess demand. Second, rationing could take place in that the number of operations given by the excess demand could be reduced for the two groups. Given some rationing rule, the demands for the operations by group R and group P, would shift in with the intersection of D_C given at the level of capacity.[202] A third possible response is that a co-payment (or user fee) could be charged for the service, denoted by p_u, which would then eliminate the excess demand. Fourth, the respective demands are a function of the quality of the operation. Reduced quality would shift in the respective demands for the operation, as well as reducing costs.

(b) Allocation by Medical Benefit

In public healthcare systems, the allocation mechanism used is often different from that employed for other private goods. In Figure 4, the demands of the two groups are based on willingness to pay. An alternative allocation is based on perceived medical benefit. This can be based on an objective of the maximization of the community's health. Wagstaff (1991) argues that the policy objective that underlies the quality-adjusted life years literature (QALY) is that "an individual's health is measured in terms of QALYs and the community's health is measured as the sum of QALYs."[203] An implication of this objective function is that medical care should be allocated to maximize total community health or aggregate medical benefit. That is, medical services should be allocated based on medical need or the expected improvement in health.

Allocation of health services according to aggregate medical benefit has the following implication. It is possible, for example, for an individual who has been recommended for surgery to have their position in the queue allocated to another person deemed to be of higher priority. It is important to realize that healthcare is one of the few areas which rely to a significant degree on this type of allocation mechanism. Another area is education, in which some private secondary schools and most post-secondary institutions admit students based on academic merit; that is, on the expected benefit of the education to be provided.

It is clear that some of the criticism directed toward public healthcare systems may be attributed to a non-acceptance of the above allocation system. While people are generally familiar with allocation by first come first served, or by willingness to pay, they may be less familiar with the allocation of healthcare by medical benefit. It may be the case that if individuals were made aware of the respective medical needs of the people in the queue, they may be willing to accept the allocation mechanism.[204] However, when no information is provided on the respective medical conditions of people in the queue, the individuals must rely on the managers of the system and trust they are following the rules of the allocation system.

(c) Conflicts in Allocation Systems

To illustrate the allocation of care by medical need, rather than using the demand curves for the two groups as in Figure 4, medical benefit curves would be constructed for the two groups, which would be summed horizontally to get the aggregate medical benefit curves. The two allocation methods for medical care would not differ if there was a perfect correlation between medical benefit and willingness to pay. However, this is unlikely to be the case. The problem occurs when the individuals who have been rationed – that is, placed on a waiting list – have a high willingness to pay for treatment. This brings the two systems into conflict. In particular, with a system based on allocation by medical need, the care received by one individual may be affected by the care required by other individuals.[205] A central source of confusion regarding healthcare issues may be that the definition of efficiency used in analyzing public health systems, at least by some healthcare observers, differs from the definition of efficiency that is commonly used by economists.[206]

(d) Redistribution

While Figure 4 is based on prices being charged for medical care, in public health systems where no explicit fees for medical treatment are levied, the excess demand is exacerbated with the total excess represented by the distance, Q_u-Q_c. To the extent that individuals are paying more in taxes than they would be charged for healthcare through premium payments, and others pay less, then the public healthcare system may really be designed for redistribution purposes.[207] This issue is separate from the term moral hazard as applied to healthcare, in that given insurance coverage, the demand for healthcare is larger than it would be in the absence of insurance.

(e) Rationing and Waiting Lists

A key issue related to the conflict of allocation systems is the type of rationing rule used when demand for care exceeds supply. There are two well-known rationing systems in the economic literature, proportional rationing and efficient rationing. Under proportional rationing everyone has the same probability of being rationed. Under efficient rationing (or parallel rationing) the available care is rationed on the basis of willingness to pay; that is, the available care is allocated to those who value it most highly. It is the outcome that would result if the consumers were costlessly able to resell the good to each other.[208]

Some of the rationing that takes place is a denial of care for medical reasons, for example surgery that either a GP or specialist deems as unnecessary. For care that is medically approved, but not received during the month, the individual's care is deferred with the individual placed on a waiting list. Waiting lists are a feature of many of the public healthcare systems examined here, in particular the Social Welfare-based systems. For example, it is reported that the average wait for elective surgery in the UK is four months, but there are wide variations in this estimate.[209]

The role of waiting lists in the healthcare market has produced a large amount of research.[210] Recently, Martin and Smith (1999) have extended the work of Lindsay and Feigenbaum (1984) and Cullis and Jones (1986) for the purposes of developing a model of the waiting list for elective surgery in the British National Health Service. A key feature of these models is that for a given a value of treatment, V, the longer the wait for treatment, the lower is this value. Specifically, the value to the individual of NHS treatment for example, is Ve^{gt} where g is the decay factor. The decay factor, as pointed out by Lindsay and Feigenbaum, represents a number of considerations including continued suffering, loss of earnings and reduced quality of life while waiting for treatment. This implies that immediate treatment is more valuable than the equivalent quality of treatment tomorrow. Martin and Smith show that the individuals who opt for private service in the UK, do so if the benefits (or utility) from private care $V-P-C$ exceeds the benefits (or utility from NHS care) $Ve^{gt}-C$, where P is the additional cost to the patient of private care, and C is the fixed cost of seeking care. It is important to note that if private care is chosen, the wait t equals zero. The model predicts that those seeking private care will be those with a relatively high g, the decay factor, given equal values of treatment V. In defining the supply side of treatment, Martin and Smith assume that future waiting time, t_1, is given as $t_1 = f(S,n,Q)$ with lower waiting times inversely related to S (the resources devoted with to surgery) and the efficiency (n) with which they are used. Higher waiting times are associated with the current queue for surgery Q.

It is important to realize that the waiting list is an integral part of a budget-constrained public healthcare system. First, as the figure indicates, it is possible with sufficient capacity that all surgery based on referrals could be performed without delay. This would mean expanding capacity beyond Q_c: with zero pricing, the amount required would be Q_u.[211] Given the fixed nature of most of the costs, a large expansion in the costs of operating the public healthcare system would be required. Other industries facing a similar peak capacity problem, such as electricity supply, use peak load pricing. In a private healthcare system, or a public health system with user fees, peak load pricing would involve a higher charge when capacity is reached. For example, economic efficiency dictates that consumers who use the service during the peak period must pay a higher rate then non-peak users.[212]

Second, if the public healthcare system has been designed to allocate care based on medical need or expected medical benefit, a queue or waiting list allows the managers of the system to decide who gets treated first. Based on reports from physicians, cases can be ranked in order of priority for treatment. This means that the healthcare managers are using not the value of the treatment to the individual, V, to allocate care but the *MB* (medical benefit) to the individual. To the extent that the individual is made to wait, the costs of waiting are privately borne. If there was sufficient capacity in the system to treat the individual in a shorter period, the costs would be publicly borne.

It is possible that some individuals diagnosed as having a less urgent need for care may never get treatment. However, if the arrival rate of urgent cases is reduced (or cyclical), the individual may eventually receive care. In some cases, healthcare officials have attempted to avoid this potential problem by developing guarantees such as the "Patient's Charter" in the UK, which has sought to guarantee that no patient should wait longer than 18 months for any surgery, and less for serious conditions.[213]

The composition of waiting lists has also received some attention in the health economics literature. Cullis and Jones (1986) report on a review of an orthopedic waiting list in the UK (L.J. Donaldson et al., 1984) which included 950 potential patients.[214] In the review, it was revealed that 20% or 190 had already been treated, and of the remaining 757, a postal questionnaire indicated that only 48% still wanted the operation. Included in the 52%, were 5% who had died, 9% who had moved away,

9% who had already received treatment, and 12% who were listed as non-respondents. The remaining 17% no longer wanted treatment. Cullis and Jones (1986) argue that the longer waiting times increased the proportion of patients no longer receiving treatment and attributed this to minor conditions being self-corrected, or for major conditions, patients too ill or frail to proceed.[215] Thus, it is clear that not all people on waiting lists will ultimately receive care, which means a lower cost incurred by the public healthcare system.

It has been observed that there are two approaches that can be used to ration health services, Locock (2000) distinguishes between implicit and explicit rationing. Implicit rationing is sometimes taken to mean rationing by clinicians, with the reason involved for the denial of care not clearly stated to anyone except (or possibly including) the person making the decisions.[216] Thus, waiting lists are an implicit mechanism because the reasoning for the delay remains private. In contrast explicit rationing makes a clear attempt to distinguish who will receive what type of care, with the decisions being understood and agreed to by a group of people, and not just the individual clinician. The well-known example of explicit rationing is the list of procedures covered in the State of Oregon health plan.[217] In examining the impact of the internal market reforms in the NHS, Locock argues that explicit rationing increased with the internal market reforms; there remains growing interest in explicit criteria to guide decision making within which clinicians exercise discretion in individual cases.[218] King and Maynard (1999) argue that the Thatcher and Blair governments in the UK have stressed supply side efficiencies in their reforms but "have not addressed the fundamental question of how to resolve the conflict between rationing based upon efficiency criteria only, and rationing that considers equity goals reflecting society's opinion of what is just and fair when choices between treatments, and inevitably between patients, are made."[219] They report that results from the Eurobarometer Survey indicates a slight majority of respondents favoring unlimited funding and unlimited service provision by the UK government. However, at the same time a significant proportion of respondents favour priorities being set, with some essential services receiving priority for NHS funding. They conclude that an open public debate on rationing is needed in the UK to facilitate the development of a health system that is clear about the values on which it is based.[220]

(f) Health Benefits Provided in Kind

A major issue of concern to supporters of a strong public role in healthcare is the fear that low-income individuals would not be able to purchase healthcare, either out-of-pocket or with health insurance. While it is possible to address this issue through income transfers to the poor, the choice is often to provide the benefit in kind. The efficacy of this approach depends on the allocation system used. If the allocation were by willingness to pay, then the benefits provided would have to replicate the distribution that would take place if income transfers were made. With sufficient income transfers, low income individuals would be able to purchase private insurance and receive care from the private sector, although depending on the prices charged by different providers, this level or quality of care might differ from that chosen by higher income individuals.

If the allocation system was designed to maximize medical benefit, the problem would be much more difficult. This kind of design would require collecting information on the expected medical benefit to all users. Once the total budget and cost of treatment were determined, the available medical care would then be allocated to those who would benefit the most.

In reality, the decision to allocate care or provide treatment is usually done on a decentralized basis by GP's deciding on whether treatment is required. If treatment is recommended, the request for treatment is then sent to the hospital and/or specialist, who receives requests for treatment from other GPs. At this stage, some decision must be made regarding which requests are acted upon. Without a centralized system to collect this information, the care is allocated by the individual specialist or group of specialists. With a centralized system, if all requests are considered of equal medical benefit, then allocation may be made on a first come first served basis. If all requests are not considered of equal medical benefit, but none are denied treatment, then a waiting list develops where less urgent, i.e., requests from GPs which are expected to yield less medical benefit, are deferred. It is clear, however, that in a highly fragmented system in which individual physicians make decisions regarding priority for treatment, it is unlikely that overall medical care is in fact being allocated to maximize medical benefit. This is separate from the issue of barriers to access to medical care, both for information and geographic reasons, which are common to all healthcare systems, both public and private.

5.2 ISSUES RELATED TO HEALTH INSURANCE

In the case of private goods purchased using insurance, there is an explicit contract governing the rights and responsibilities of the parties to the contract, the insurance company and the insured individual. In some Social Welfare-based health systems, no explicit healthcare premium is charged and often there is some uncertainty regarding what medical care is covered by the public insurer.[221] In order to place a number of healthcare issues into perspective, it is important to define the alternative insurance policies that can be and are used.

As pointed out by Arrow (1963:962), three different methods of health insurance coverage for medical costs have been historically used: (1) prepayment – which provides an unlimited amount of covered services in return for a fixed predetermined premium, (2) indemnities according to a fixed schedule – which provides for cash payments to the beneficiary contingent on the particular medical condition which are fixed in advance and (3) insurance against costs – which also involves cash payments to the beneficiary, in which the carrier pays all the costs, whatever they might be, subject to provisions like deductibles and coinsurance.[222] It should be noted that deductibles and coinsurance can be used together. For example, in the event of illness, the policy may not cover the first $500 of costs – the deductible – which is covered out of pocket, and beneficiaries might have to pay a coinsurance rate of (for example) 20% of each additional dollar in charges. It is important to note that some choice is generally available for the extent of coverage, in that for a range of premiums, individuals can buy a range of coverage.

(a) Adverse Selection

There are two important economic issues that arise when risks are covered by insurance. The first is *adverse selection*, which is the result of information known by the potential insurance purchaser but hidden from the insurer. For example, individuals seeking insurance may have a pre-existing medical condition, or know that they are relatively more likely to develop a particular disease or illness due to family history. If the insurance company offers a menu of insurance policies for both high risks and low risks and is unable to distinguish ex ante between the types, then the policy meant for high risks will not be chosen: everyone will choose the low-risk, premium/coverage combination. In this case, the insurance company would lose money. This problem would also occur if a monopoly insurer tried to set an average premium/coverage combination when entry is allowed. The entering firm would be able to offer a premium/coverage combination which would attract low risk types and cause the monopoly "pooling" contract to lose money.[223] This is referred to as cream-skimming.

This issue is important in thinking about the role of potential competition in the health insurance market. One response to the adverse selection problem is to have community rating rather than experience rating. Experience rating is done at the individual level, and attempts are made to sort individuals by their risk class with a premium/coverage combination being offered to the particular risk class. In particular it has been argued by Tobin (1996) that "if everyone is to have and to be compelled to have insurance for a common basic package of services, independently of ability to pay and of state of health, then clearly the insurers cannot be allowed to select risks or charge premiums."[224]

Community rating would involve estimating the potential costs (payouts) and potential premiums required to insure a particular group of individuals. This can also be coupled with a compulsory requirement as, for example, with Blue Cross Dental plans for a company or organization. A key issue is that if community rating is done at the company or employment level, then risk characteristics may differ by company, and in particular, would differ from the unemployed and the elderly. However, Tobin (1996) argues that the principle of community rating could be implemented. The method is as follows.[225] The risks facing an insurer are a function of the risk characteristics of its pool. A policy of risk equalization could be implemented whereby insurers with lower risks in their clientele than some national representative sample would have to pay into an equalization pool, which would go to insurers with higher risk characteristics. Tobin argues that it is important that the payments be based on advance or (ex ante) risk assessments.

The possibility of insurers competing based on common types of coverage is evident in the German healthcare system. Furthermore, private insurers compete on the basis of community rating in Australia.[226] Community rating in Australia requires that private insurers not discriminate between contributors on the basis of health status, age, race, gender, sexuality, use of hospital or medical services, or general claims history. To support the principle of community rating, a system of reinsurance exists within the private health insurance industry. As described by Tobin (1996), insurers with a greater proportion of low risk members (generally the young) pay contributions into the reinsurance pool, while those with a greater proportion of high risk groups (the chronically ill and the aged) draw funds from the pool.

It has been suggested that the use of community rating in Australia was a factor in the decline in the purchase of private health insurance prior to the changes in 1999. Hopkins and Frech III (2001) argue that community rating distorts the market for private insurance because it makes the insurance expensive and unattractive for low risk consumers (particularly the young) and inexpensive and attractive for high risk consumers (particularly the elderly). They argue that in practice community rating usually makes insurance less attractive overall.[227] Furthermore, they state that in Australia, membership declined and the pool of persons privately insured increasingly consisted of the high risk and elderly, and became less attractive to private insurers.

They argue that the change in the application of community rating under the National Health Amendment Act of 1999 to include a "Lifetime Health Cover" appears to explain most of the increase in insurance coverage. The change introduced a limited amount of age rating into private health insurance, and was designed to provide a strong incentive to remain insured once one joins the system.[228] This would prevent what Hopkins and Frech III call "hit and run" behaviour, which happens when individuals only join the plan when they anticipate using private hospital treatment and withdraw from the fund once the treatment has been completed. On the base of evidence they were able to gather, Hopkins and Frech III (2001) conclude that the increase in private insurance coverage and subsequent increase in private hospital activity reduced the waiting times in the public hospital sector, which is often what motivates governments to subsidize private health insurance. They recognize that a key policy issue in Australia is whether the large government subsidy of private health insurance is necessary or efficient. Also, some Australians are concerned that the changes have created considerable gains for both private hospitals and private health insurance funds.[229]

(b) Moral Hazard

The other issue is *moral hazard*. Moral hazard results from what is called hidden action; One party to a contract can take actions that are not observed by the other party which effects the terms of trade of the contract. For example, suppose someone is seeking house insurance.[230] If the premium charged could reflect the level of care taken in preventing fire or theft, then the first best insurance contract could be obtained. However, when this is not possible, alternatives such as coinsurance or deductibles are included in contracts to protect the insurer against some types of moral hazard. The extent to which coinsurance or deductibles are valuable depends on the prevalence of moral hazard related to the particular medical service. The more prevalent the overuse, the more insurance or deductibles can limit the misallocation of resources. In terms of healthcare coverage, the demand side instruments – deductibles or user fees – are more important in reducing moral hazard, the more likely is the overuse of the particular medical treatment.

(c) Extent of Coverage

In any insurance contract, the premium charged is related to the nature and type of risks that are to be covered. In the healthcare area, one can imagine a range of coverage, from comprehensive which includes all health risks to limited coverage confined to supplementary costs such as the cost of a private room and pharmaceuticals.

It is also possible to have these risks insured wholly by the public sector or partly by the public and private sectors as is case with supplementary insurance in Canada. It is also possible in principle to have all but elective surgery covered by the public health sector, with private premiums covering the costs of elective surgery. In this case, it is important to be able to discern whether the care required is acute or elective. As might be expected, the insurance premiums are positively related to the extent of the coverage, with lower premiums being charged for lower coverage.

(d) Tax Credits and Medical Savings Accounts

In the US, it has been suggested that one approach to the reform of healthcare could be to use tax credits and medical savings accounts. Pauly and Goodman (1995) argue that the current system of private insurance in the US offers more favourable tax treatment to citizens who obtain their insurance through employment, since the employer-provided benefit is excluded from federal income and payroll taxation. In addition, this subsidy is unavailable to the employed, employees of firms without such coverage, and the self-employed.

Pauly and Goodman (1995) propose tax credits for the purchase of combinations of catastrophic coverage and what are called "Medical Savings Account" (MSAs).[231] The idea behind MSAs is to provide an earmarked savings account to pay for small medical bills and to offer rewards for prudent decisions. Specifically, they "propose a tax credit to help all families pay for insurance and finance their MSAs. It offers a specific dollar reduction in taxes (or a refund or voucher, if the family owes no taxes) for those families who obtain at least catastrophic coverage."[232] The tax credit would be a fixed dollar or predetermined amount. It would work as follows. With the higher deductible which would accompany a shift away from full coverage to catastrophic coverage only, the premium could be substantially reduced. This reduced premium would be deposited in a MSA account. This would be the account which is used to pay for minor medical expenses. According to Pauly and Goodman (1995), while this shift would increase the expected value of expenses below the deductible, savings in this system would come from the new incentives not to use excess care.[233] The better incentive comes largely from the fact that people may be able to withdraw unused funds for other purposes at the end of any insurance year.

(e) Competition at the Insurance Level

It is important to note that competition at the insurance level provides a number of functions. First, a competitive private insurance firm must ensure that its total cost of providing insurance equals its total revenues. The firm has an interest in monitoring the costs of providing insurance, including the prices charged by physicians, hospitals and other health-care professionals. It must do this while keeping in mind that the patients expect a certain level of care consistent with their contracts. If the firm does not do an adequate job of monitoring costs, then its total premiums would have to go up, which if it faces competition from other insurance firms, would result in fewer subscribers and lower revenues. Similarly, if the firm tries to limit coverage below the contracted amount, it will also lose subscribers. In both cases, the survival of the firm depends on its monitoring ability. Thus competition plays a key role in enhancing efficiency. In the case of a monopoly insurer, either public or private, this implicit monitoring function which competition provides, must be replicated in some other way either through planning or regulation.

(f) Costs of Multiple Insurers

It should be noted that a common criticism of private health insurance is the cost of administering the variety of health plans. It is argued that a public insurer avoids this problem because of its use of a single plan.

Presumably, this efficiency would also occur with a monopoly private insurer. It should be noted, though, that the benefits of monitoring providers do not disappear with a single public insurer, although it may have less incentive to do so. The reason is that if the public insurer is the sole provider of insurance, then it has the ability to raise premiums for all insurers sufficiently to cover the higher costs that result from the reduced monitoring. However, faced with a global budget constraint, the public insurer will have some incentive to monitor although, it usually has greater degrees of freedom to cover higher costs.

The administrative costs related to private health insurance result from the diversity of healthcare plans offered. If a standard health insurance plan for private insurers were specified, then this would be similar to a standard public insurance plan. While involving lower administrative costs, the uniform private health insurance plan results in a loss of benefits to consumers that come from a diversity of health insurance plans.

There is an empirical literature that discusses the relative benefits of a single insurer. Woolhandler, Campbell and Himmelstein (2003) estimate the relative administrative costs for providing healthcare between Canada and the United States. They estimate that for 1999, health-administration costs in the U.S. amounted to $294.3 billion (U.S. dollars) with the respective per capita costs for the United States being $1,059 and $307 for Canada.[234] Woolhandler et al. attribute the difference to the costs of running a private insurance system – including underwriting and marketing – that are absent in the Canadian system. They also state that a system with multiple insurers, multiple claims and multiple processing facilities as well as smaller insured groups is more costly than a single insurer Canadian system. They point out that "fragmentation also raises costs for providers who must deal with multiple insurance products – at least 755 in Seattle alone – forcing them to determine an applicant's eligibility and to keep track of the various copayments, referral networks and approval requirements."[235] Aaron (2003) argues that the analysis of Woolhandler et al (2003) seriously overstates the differences in administrative costs between the two systems, and that the apparent increased bang for the healthcare buck in Canada may be due more to the regulation of physician fees and the use of global budgets to control hospital spending in Canada.[236] In addition, it is unclear whether the real issue is not the diversity of health insurance plans but rather the number of insurers per se. A single type of health insurance plan, as exists in Canada, has its administrative advantages, but presumably results in a loss of welfare due to lack of diversity in the type of health plans available. Private sector firms offer a menu of coverage/premium combinations to satisfy these differing demands. Presumably a movement from a U.S. style system to a Canadian style healthcare system would have to include these welfare "losses."

5.3 ISSUES RELATED TO COMPETITION BETWEEN HEALTHCARE PROVIDERS

(a) Autonomy of Healthcare Providers and the Cost of Healthcare Services

Figure 2 illustrates the market for health services, featuring specialist healthcare providers and general practitioners who have much more autonomy than do specialist workers in other sectors. Specialist workers in other sectors are often paid a salary, or in some cases, such as law or accounting firms, they receive a share of the firm's profits. Specialists in healthcare or general practitioners are often more like independent contractors, or owner/managers.

Within a competitive market of private firms, the owner/manager chooses inputs to provide the good or service at least cost. In doing so, the owner/manager chooses to hire inputs until the value of the input's marginal product equals the cost of the input. Where there are alternative combinations of inputs to provide the good or service, this means that the mix of inputs used will differ depending on their marginal productivities and costs. With regard to healthcare, to the extent that inputs are substitutes – drugs, therapy, surgery or hospital care – an owner/manager of an integrated healthcare firm would choose the appropriate treatment (inputs) depending on the cost and productivity of each of the inputs into medical care.[237]

This process is made difficult when each of the input owners has independent producer status. Each provider may not take into account the costs imposed on other providers and may not be aware of other treatments that are less costly. In cases where the costs of alternative types of treatment are known to other providers, there may be no economic incentive to outline these options to patients. Moreover, specialist workers in other firms are usually charged for complementary inputs as, for example, with an accountant who uses an office to operate his or her practice. The complementary inputs are most often privately owned. Complementary inputs for surgeons are hospital services, which are often publicly financed. Surgeons are not charged for these hospital inputs. That is, hospitals are quite different from private sector firms and are more like publicly funded institutions which provide complementary inputs for independent contractors.[238] A solution to this problem, one used in other industries, is to establish an integrated firm, or partnership, which allows the least cost choice of inputs to be used to produce the good or service. In the healthcare sector, this would involve healthcare firms, in which physicians, nurses, pharmaceuticals, and hospital facilities are all used to provide healthcare in the most cost-effective manner.

(b) Differences in Objectives for Hospitals and Insurers

In comparing Figure 1 and Figure 2, it is important to emphasize that the objectives of hospital managers may differ depending on whether they manage public firms or private companies. Similarly, the objectives of insurers, whether they are public or private, may differ. In particular, managers of publicly-managed or owned companies face different incentives than managers of privately-owned firms. Private for-profit insurers must keep costs down to meet the expectations of owners and shareholders. Monopoly public insurers have more degrees of freedom regarding pricing and coverage. All that is required for a monopoly public insurer is that the total revenues (possibly financed by premiums) equal total costs to serve all types of risk classes. This constraint allows for a considerable degree of cross-subsidization, which is in general more difficult if the managers face competition from other insurers.

(c) Differences in Cost Conditions

The cost conditions governing the provision of health services may differ in important ways from the cost conditions governing the provision of other private goods. In general, the efficient market structure in terms of the number of firms, or in this case the number of hospitals, is dependent on the cost function governing the production of the good or service (including transportation costs) in relation to the level of demand for health services.

In thinking about the cost function for health services, it is important to distinguish between economies of scale and economies of scope. Economies of scale are defined as the cost savings from large scale production. For example, suppose the average cost of a hip replacement decreases as the number of hip replacement is performed in a clinic or hospital. If the savings, in average costs, are eventually exhausted, then there is a minimum efficient scale for hip replacements: an output level at which average costs are at a minimum.[239]

Dranove (1998) identifies several potential sources of scale economies in hospitals, with many related to the spreading of fixed capital. For example, as a medical records department grows, the hospital may substitute computers for personnel. The fixed costs of computers, if spread over a larger number of patients, will result in lower average costs. Similar economies may result from the fixed costs of supervisory personnel. Another source of scale economies, according to Dranove, is the economies of massed reserves – or the more efficient use of capacity. For example, a hospital that is large enough for only one MRI may need to hold it idle much of the time to permit emergency testing, whereas a larger hospital with two MRIs may need to schedule less idle time as a percentage of total available time.[240]

In addition to these production costs we must add transportation costs. For example, production costs may be minimized for a large number of operations, but if this means increased costs borne by patients, in particular increased costs for travel and accommodation, then this would limit the particular size of the clinic or hospital that would be consistent with overall efficiency. Including the costs of travel provides one rationale for having more clinics or hospitals than is consistent with *production efficiency*, where costs of travel are excluded. Note, however, that if the public system has fewer hospitals or clinics than is consistent with the overall total costs, including transportation costs, then part of the cost of providing health services has been shifted to the patients, who bear the private cost of travel and accommodation.

"Economies of scope" is a different concept. The term refers to the cost saving that occurs when more than one output or activity is produced by a firm. For example, suppose the total costs of 20 hip replacements and 20 knee surgeries are lower if both are performed in the same hospital or clinic instead of being done in separate clinics. The source of this saving might be a sharing of overhead or staff related to both procedures. If economies of scope exist for a number of procedures, this gives a rationale for them to be done in the same location, either a clinic or hospital.

Folland et al. (1997) discuss the recent empirical literature examining economies of scope in the delivery of healthcare services. The studies differ somewhat in their definition of multiple services and their conclusions regarding economies of scope. For example, Dunn et al. (1995) find there are economies of scope from the performance of more than one surgery on the same day. They found that doing two procedures in one surgery reduces total work by 22% compared to separate surgeries.[241] Fourier and Mitchell (1992) examined 179 short-term general care hospitals in Florida and found that statistically significant economies of scope were estimated among various categories of services.[242]

Why are these two concepts so important? The reason is that they can provide some guidance to determine whether free entry of firms would result in a close to optimal market structure. First, consider economies of scale. For the case where market demand is large and the minimum efficient scale is low, it is desirable that a relatively large number of firms exist in the market. For the case where market demand is low, and the minimum efficient scale is large, then efficiency may dictate fewer firms (hospitals or clinics) than would exist under free entry. Suppose economies of scale are large in relation to transportation costs. This means that large-scale clinics or hospitals are the preferred arrangement, which would suggest a concentration of procedures in a few clinics or hospitals. If economies of scope are small or nonexistent, this means that single procedures can be provided by clinics or hospitals specializing in, say, cataract surgery. Second, where economies of scope are present, it is optimal to have firms provide multiple products or multiple services. When applied to medical care, this means that there may be cost savings from having more than one medical treatment take place in one hospital or private facility. That is, the optimal provider of health services may be a multiproduct firm or a full service hospital.

However, even when economies of scope exist, it does not mean that public provision is necessarily required, since it is possible that private provision can occur subject to price and/or entry regulation. That is, even in the case of natural monopoly – single-firm production being optimal – Demsetz (1968) argues that franchise bidding or other contractual arrangements to provide service is possible and feasible in some cases.[243]

(d) Differences in Competitive Conditions

There is often little or no competition between hospitals. This may be the result of previous planning decisions, or the result of scale economies. One key factor restraining the market area of hospitals, though, is the importance of transportation costs. Transportation costs naturally limit the scale that might be reached by a hospital in the absence of transportation costs. This is simply because farther travel for patients might jeopardize their health, in the case of emergencies, as well as increasing transportation costs for both patients and their families. It is important to note though that within this local area, the hospital may have some market power. The introduction of competitive forces at the hospital stage was the goal of Britain's "internal market", where it was hoped that competition between providers would increase efficiency.

(e) Costs and Medical Output

A important issue is the determination of the costs of medical procedures, in particular where there are common fixed costs. This issue arises in a number of other industries. In general, two common approaches are used to price the output of goods produced with a common fixed cost. The first is called Fully Distributed Cost pricing, in which the fixed costs are allocated based on some measure of usage. For example, the costs of long distance versus local service might be allocated based on the fraction of calls that are long distance. The second is called Ramsey pricing, in which the outputs of the respective services are reduced in some proportionate manner. This reduction in output results in prices higher than marginal costs, which provides the necessary total revenues in order to cover total costs, including fixed costs.

Even if this issue is resolved, there is still the question of measuring the output and quality of a healthcare system.[244] There is a feeling among some healthcare observers that what makes the health market unique is the difficulty involved in determining the output of the industry. For example, one measure might be the total number of elective surgeries done per physician. A second measure might be how many patients were satisfied with the treatment. A third measure might be the number of readmissions, that is the number of individuals who have returned for treatment for the same medical condition. Finally, higher output might mean cost effectiveness. The problem of quality measurement of an output is not unique to health services. Many services face this issue, for example, education, legal or investment services; however, these services have had a long history of private provision.

The number of medical procedures must also be calibrated to the objective of the healthcare system. In a system where the objective is to maximize medical benefit subject to a budget constraint, maximizing the number of surgeries may not be optimal. This is particularly true if what has been called supplier induced demand (SID) is present. SID is related to the information problem. Doctors may be able to convince patients that a particular treatment or prescription is needed when in fact it is unnecessary.

Recently, Grytten and Sørenson (2001) examined the issue of type of contract and supplier-induced demand for primary physicians in Norway. They compared the response of fee-for-service primary physicians with salaried physicians to variations in demand for primary-care physician services. They conclude that "we did not find SID for primary physician services in Norway."[245] Furthermore, they state that this finding is consistent with some of the more recent literature within this field. They argue that previous work that has found SID to be based on aggregated data from geographic units, data which suffers "because the theoretical inducement model describes factors associated with the physician's behaviour rather than variation in consumption of physician services per capita."[246] Similarly, Folland et al. (1997) argue that "elements of competition, agency relationships, and consumer search place substantial limits on the ability and willingness of physicians to generate increases in demand. .... Therefore it seems safe to suggest that healthcare markets can often be studied using models that postulate stable demand functions even though there may be some degree of SID."[247]

5.4 ISSUES RELATED TO TOTAL FUNDING OF THE SYSTEM

(a) Demand side versus Supply Side Control Mechanisms

The health economics literature distinguishes between demand-side policies and supply-side policies as approaches governments use to influence the allocation of resources in the healthcare sector. Demand-side policies include co-payments, user fees, deductibles, and in general any fee that is paid by the users of healthcare in order to access health services. Supply side policies include fixed hospital budgets, which may include capitation payments for physicians, or a limit on the number and type of hospital beds. They also include a restriction on the availability of technology, or the types of prescription drugs that are available, or any policy that affects the total supply of health services in an area.

In terms of demand-side policies, an ongoing public policy issue is the effect that charges to consumers have on the access to medical care, particularly low income individuals. This is separate from the issue of differential access to health services in terms of geography or knowledge of medical issues. Apart from the issue of limiting access, it has been suggested that the use of demand side policies, in particular differential fees for service, can play a useful role in providing signals of the relative cost of services. For example, higher fees for inpatient hospital care versus outpatient care can direct users of healthcare to lower-cost options.

Public healthcare advocates who dislike the market-like approach of demand side policies often see supply side policies as the preferred method of allocating healthcare resources. It is this direct restriction on choice, often manifested by large waiting lists for elective surgery, which then becomes the source of complaints by many people that the public health system is inadequate.

(b) Global Cost Conditions

In general, total expenditure on a particular good or service is often not a public policy concern, unless it is related to some particular social objective. For example, there is little or no concern that a country's total expenditure on education as a fraction of GDP is excessive.[248]

In public healthcare systems it is often stated that centralized control or administration is effective in lowering overall costs of the healthcare system. This is often discussed in the context of the share of GDP spent on health. Public systems that feature centralized bargaining over salaries of physicians, nurses and other healthcare participants are often successful in lowering or restraining costs.[249] Coupled with a restriction or limitation on supplementary or private expenditures, this can lead to lower total healthcare spending, both public and private. Often overlooked, however, is that fact that if a global cost-control strategy results in long waiting lists for elective surgery, significant welfare costs associated with the queue are incurred by individuals on the list. For example, Bishai and Lang (2000) estimate the loss in consumer surplus due to the length of the queue for cataract surgery for patients in Manitoba, Denmark and Barcelona. These non-budgetary hidden costs are estimated to be 0.05%, 0.0177% and 0.01% of the total health spending in Canada, Denmark and Spain for cataract surgery alone. According to Bishai and Lang, these estimates represent the societal gains that could be achieved in each country if waiting time could be reduced holding marginal costs constant.[250]

It is clear that a global cost constraint is not pursued for any other good or service, and is often justified by a concern for reducing unnecessary medical procedures. For example, it may be felt that if fewer resources were provided for healthcare, managers and healthcare professionals would be forced to allocate their resources to maximize medical benefit. The public policy merit of this strategy obviously depends on the prevalence of unnecessary medical procedures, and whether the strategy is effective as a tool to enhance efficiency.

The reason that total expenditure on healthcare is an issue, is that it affects the budgets of governments in Social Welfare systems, or the costs of healthcare by employers and labour in Social Insurance health systems. For example, in France, where premiums are paid by employers and employees, cost containment is pursued for competitive reasons, that is, as a way to ensure that domestic costs do not rise at a rate which makes the products sold internationally less competitive. Where the total budget and hence taxes are affected by the total costs of healthcare, incumbent governments feel pressure to maintain stable tax rates as way of demonstrating good government. It is for this reason that public health systems with alternative methods of financing, distanced somewhat from government control, are often in a better position to respond to the increased demands for some health services. Social-Insurance-based systems seem to have a clear advantage in this regard. The arm's length nature of the insurer insulates governments somewhat from making the direct political choice between higher taxes or lower levels of services.

A significant issue that arises in largely publicly-funded health systems is how to deal with the requests from private individuals to purchase supplementary health insurance. It has been pointed out that this is really an equity issue. Tobin (1996) argues that the key issue is the elasticity of supply of the medical treatment in question. For example, if the supply of the activity can be increased at constant costs, and basic services are still covered by what he terms the standard package, Tobin states "it makes no sense to say that rich people may spend their wealth on yachts and diamonds but not on cosmetic surgery and orthodontics."[251] The issue is that if there are no scarce factors, then the additional services demanded and supplied to higher income individuals does not affect the availability of services to the lower income individuals. In should be noted that if the increase in the demand for health services is privately funded then the total public spending on the medical activity may stay constant but the overall total spending on the activity may rise. This conflicts with the notion of a global cost constraint on total healthcare spending.

It has been suggested that allowing the existence of a parallel private healthcare system weakens the public healthcare system. Doyal and Doyal (1999) feel that as the underfunding of the NHS in Britain continues, that more people will turn to the private healthcare system. They argue that this group will be less willing to support the public system through increased taxes. While acknowledging that eliminating the private sector in the UK health system would be politically unrealistic, they feel that if everyone had to depend on the same healthcare system, "there is little doubt that current levels of care within the NHS would improve."[252] In contrast, Cullis and Jones (1985) argue that the introduction of a parallel private healthcare system, providing the same type of health services as the public system, can result in a reduction in the costs imposed on the public system. Cullis and Jones argue that given a zero user cost, the total demand for elective surgeries, is made up of three components, the demand served by the private sector, the demand served by the public sector, and the unmet demand which is the waiting list. Any expansion of the demand served by the private sector, for example by a subsidy, can reduce the demand placed on the public sector and can lower waiting lists.[253] In fact, they argue that a subsidy for private purchase of healthcare releases resources from the public sector which can then be devoted to shortening the waiting list, at a lower total cost, than would an expansion of the public sector budget and a prohibition on the private sector.

A significant issue in the global cost condition debate is what contributes to the expanding demands on the healthcare budget. Here a number of explanations have been offered. The first is that as a society becomes wealthier it generally chooses to devote an increasing share of total GNP or spending to healthcare. Formally, healthcare is a luxury good.[254] The second is that the price indexes may be misleading in that the higher budget may really mean higher quality of care. The third is what has been termed the "Cost Disease" or "Baumol's Law" of labour provided services. Baumol (1993) has argued that it is not surprising that certain services like healthcare face rising costs over time. The reason is that when a service is produced with a large labour input whose productivity can not be easily enhanced, the cost of the service will rise in relation to the cost of providing other goods and services where technology is more readily able to increase labour productivity. The higher productivity of labour in the non-service sector gets reflected in higher wages overall including the service sector, which means relatively stagnant productivity and higher wages over time in the healthcare and other service sectors. According to Baumol (1993), one reason for the stagnant productivity growth in healthcare and education is that in both cases the service resists standardization.[255] For example, medical treatment must be tailored to the individual patient or student. The second reason according to Baumol is that the quality of these services is often related to the amount of labour time applied, for example, the length of consultation with a doctor, or the amount of individual teacher attention. For these reasons, Baumol (1993) concludes that "if my analysis is correct, a difficult choice will be required; either ever more of gross national product will have to be channeled through the public sector, with all the problems we know that to entail; or alternatively, these services will have to be transferred to private enterprise, in fields where private business firms can hope to succeed only if granted an immunity from temptation of unwise government interference."[256]

(c) Sources of Funding

A significant issue for publicly funded healthcare systems is the political ramifications that emerge depending on how the system is financed. In Social Welfare-based systems, like the UK, the government pays for public healthcare out of general revenues. In general, in these systems, there is no explicit targeting of funds for healthcare, as is done for Employment Insurance and the Canada Pension Plan.[257] Thus, individuals see only the total tax bill. It remains opaque to taxpayers as to whether a tax increase will go for improved healthcare, or increased general government spending, which might be valuable or wasted. It seems clear that a first step is to have an explicit accounting of the amount of taxes going to healthcare be made known to individuals. Opponents of this view argue that if the full tax cost of the public healthcare system was made known to individuals, then there might actually be less support for the public system.

Alternatives to a total reliance on general revenues involve some private payment, either co-payments (a price per visit perhaps covered by private insurance) or a yearly health premium (lump sum charge to households), along with tax deductions at source by the various levels of government. The latter can include matching contributions by employers. The advantage of a multiple financing system is that it allows more flexibility in funding. For example, it would be possible to increase the user fee, yearly premium or tax rates separately, all of which would have different efficiency and equity components. Such a funding scheme would allow healthcare issues to be separated from other political issues.

(d) Planning versus Contracting

A key issue in the healthcare systems reviewed here is the intellectual and practical debate between increased planning or an increased use of contracts to improve the performance of the system. Those generally opposed to the use of contracts believe improvements in the healthcare system can be achieved by better planning and improved administrative efforts, including exchanges of best practices and more extensive use of data. Those in favour of alternative approaches are more pessimistic that increased centralization of information and control can make a significant difference. They generally put more faith in nongovernment organizations, either private not-for-profit or for-profit firms. An advantage of non-government control over resources is that changes to the structure of the system are generally decentralized, and are easier to make. A disadvantage, is that supporters of a strong public role feel they have less influence on the resulting structure. In other industries, this influence is generally exerted through regulatory agencies rather than through explicit political means.

A significant impediment to the use of contracts with private providers is the lack of information on the existing costs of medical procedures incurred by public departments or health authorities. As pointed out by Enthoven in his analysis of the NHS, if the internal cost of a procedure is unknown, it makes it difficult for public managers to make effective use of private providers. This problem is exacerbated, in general, the larger the number of medical procedures that are currently being provided by the respective hospitals.

CHAPTER VI

ISSUES IN THE REGULATION OF A PRIVATE HEALTHCARE SECTOR

A number of suggested policy options have the effect of introducing "private" market-like features into a publicly funded healthcare system. They include the following.

6.1 COMPETITION AT THE INSURANCE LEVEL

It is important to discuss the nature of competition at the insurer level. As has been seen, it is possible to have a monopoly public insurer like the UK and Swedish systems, or a number of competing nonprofit insurers like Germany and Belgium. For example, in countries with a Social Welfare-based health system, such as the UK and Sweden, taxes which are used to fund the public healthcare system all go to either the Department of Health in the UK or the respective County Council in Sweden. In countries with an insurance-based public healthcare system such as Germany, individuals can choose a particular health insurance fund, while in Belgium and in France the funds involve an arm's length public organization whose job is to operate the healthcare system. In contrast, private insurance in the US is supplied by a large number of for-profit insurers. In the countries in this study, supplementary insurance can be provided by private firms as in the UK or as an additional option available from the mutualité as in France or from the SHI in Germany.

A problem that exists in Social Welfare-based systems is that there is no separate insurer whose tasks are to ensure that patients receive the care to which they are entitled, as well as to monitor the costs of care being provided. This is all done within a single department or County Council. The problem is that a conflict of interest can exist when healthcare decisions are not made by an arm's length organization from government, in particular, when there is a monopoly public insurer. To the extent that expenditure control is a priority of government, this can conflict with ensuring that all patients have access to the required care. This is a particularly important issue when high cost care is required.

When the competitive constraint on the insurance function is eliminated, it is critical to somehow replicate the implicit monitoring of the insurance contract and provider cost that is provided by competition. The extent to which such systems have been successful is a matter of debate.

To understand the above issues, it is helpful to consider the case of a monopoly public insurer providing automobile insurance. For example, in a number of provinces, like Manitoba, a public insurer – a Crown Corporation – is the sole provider of automobile insurance in the province. In this case, all vehicle owners who wish to operate a vehicle must purchase insurance from the public corporation. The premiums are related to the risk of the insured, although it has been argued that there is less variation in premiums than under private automobile insurance systems.[258] If someone is involved in an automobile accident, the individual takes his automobile – if it can be driven – to an adjuster at one of a number of claim centers.[259] The damage is assessed and if it appears that the damage is covered by the insurance contract, the automobile owner is given permission to approach a number of *private* auto body shops for repair. The costs of the repairs, subject to a deductible, are then paid to the auto body shop by the public insurer.

An issue that often arises in this setting is the role of the adjustor. Given the adjustor is employed by the insurer, it appears that the adjustor is in a conflict of interest. Should the payouts be too generous, the total payouts of insurers and hence the bottom line would be effected. It would seem that the adjustor would be under pressure to make relatively modest payouts. For example, certain high-cost payouts to accident victims could be kept at modest levels to reduce the costs to the corporation. On the other hand, it is possible that higher payouts to claimants could be passed onto other automobile owners. Given its monopoly position, it is much easier for the corporation to pass on the increased costs than if it faced competition from other insurers.

To address the potential conflict of interest, public auto insurers often have an appeal process which is designed to be a neutral arbitrator of disputes. To make the parallel with a monopoly public-health insurer, this would mean that the General Practitioners/Specialists would be public employees on salary, who would then face pressures similar to those faced by the public-insurance adjustor. The point is that once a monopoly insurer is in place, the issue of ensuring that the monopoly deals fairly with claimants becomes crucial.

In most discussions of a parallel private/public healthcare system, there seems to be a concern that the introduction of a private sector will result in relatively large profits for the private sector, which will increase the costs of the public sector. The common term is "cream skimming" in that the private sector will only insure the relatively healthy segment of the population. If choice is given to consumers to opt out of the public system, then the "good" risks will depart, leaving a relatively "poor health" group for the public system. In normal insurance markets, private insurance companies spend a great deal of time and effort attempting to identify the risk class of the individual. In a competitive insurance market, higher risk individuals must be charged higher premiums than low risk individuals if the insurer is to break even. In some cases, the private insurance scheme has been replaced by a public corporation, such as Manitoba Public Insurance Corporation in Manitoba (MPIC). It is important to realize that governments can regulate private-sector firms in order to avoid problems that may occur with private sector entry.

In Social Welfare-based healthcare systems, in which a uniform deductible or no explicit premiums are charged, all individuals are insured, with funding for the system coming out of general revenues. In reality, higher-income individuals will pay higher levels of local, regional, or federal income taxes which go to support the publicly funded healthcare system. Thus, if high-income individuals are lower risks, that is, are healthier than low income individuals, then the high income individuals are cross subsidizing the risks of the low income individuals.

A number of policy alternatives exist in order to introduce a parallel private-insurance system within a predominantly public insurance system. These alternatives are related to the question of whether individuals choosing the private system should be allowed to opt out of the public system, as in Germany. If they are allowed to opt out, a number of possiblities exist. Individuals opting for private insurance could have some, all, or none of the taxes – income, payroll, sales – they currently pay for public healthcare refunded in order to purchase coverage from the private sector. This would be similar to how private education is treated in many Canadian provinces. Alternatives range from full funding of separate schools to partial funding of private education.[260]

A system of opting out could be implemented in principle by providing individuals who opt out of the public system with a type of medical care voucher. The amount of the voucher could be all or a fraction of the taxes paid in support of the public healthcare system. If high income individuals are allowed to opt out of the publicly funded system, but are not allowed to take their tax liabilities with them, (i.e., no voucher system), then they would pay for both the public system and the private system. This would obviously lower the incentive to choose the private alternative. If individuals who choose private healthcare are required to also support the public system, this would be similar to how private education is treated in many provinces in Canada. That is, individuals must support the public system, through property taxes or income taxes, as well as pay the cost of private education. Individuals who chose to opt out of the public system could be restricted completely from using the public system or could have their use of the public system restricted to some types of services. As can be seen, there is considerable flexibility available to governments should they decide to allow for the coexistence of a parallel private healthcare sector.

6.2 COMPETITION AT THE PROVIDER STAGE

A principal goal of the creation of an "internal" market in the UK public healthcare system was to create competition between the providers of healthcare. In Diagram 1, this would involve competition between "hospitals" or, in the UK case, trusts. The objective was to have the competition lower costs through reducing the claims on the public purse.

(a) Yardstick competition

A key question that arises is the objective of introducing a parallel system. Is it to have the private sector provide what is called "yardstick" competition? That is, given that the public as represented by the government may not know the true costs of providing public healthcare, it may be advantageous to have a profit-maximizing private sector for comparisons. There are several examples of services provided by the private sector that are similar to the services provided by the public sector. For example, in Canada CN and CP competed in rail transportation, Air Canada and Canadian Airlines competed in airline transportation, and even the CBC and the private networks compete in television programming. Alternatively, is the role of the public system to provide subsidized healthcare, in order to constrain the prices charged by the private sector? In Diagram 1, this would imply that some of the hospitals would be private, and some would be public. Such a system would be consistent with maintaining a single public insurer, or parallel private and public insurance systems.

(b) Relationship of the Private Sector to the Public Sector

There are a number of alternatives that arise when one considers the introduction of a private healthcare system in a dominant public healthcare system. At one extreme, the private sector could be completely divorced from the public sector. Resources employed in the private sector – physicians and nurses and hospital services – could be operated independently from the public system. Healthcare firms could be structured as partnerships or limited-liability companies that would be responsible for paying all costs incurred in providing healthcare. All payments received would be privately funded either out of pocket or through private insurance.

Alternatively, one could imagine that physicians, nurses and other hospital staff as well as hospital services could be devoted partly to private patients, while still receiving funds from the public based on services provided in support of the public healthcare system. This occurs in the UK system. The fees that are charged the public patients in private hospitals could be regulated with any additional costs incurred by publicly financed patients in private hospitals financed either out of pocket or through supplementary private insurance.

A related concern is that all the "high quality" doctors will then work in the private system, either completely separate from the public system, or else devote more of their time and energies to their private practice. As observed by Propper (2000), in systems like UK, where labour is employed in both the NHS and the private sector, a significant expansion in private demand for healthcare will reduce the availability of staff to the public sector and to reduce the quality of public services, at least in the short run.[261] It is clear that any proposed expansion in the private sector would require an expansion in the supply of all healthcare personnel in order to avoid this problem.[262]

This concern – over the possible loss of "high quality" doctors from the public system – has merit if there is substantial variation in the competence or skill of doctors. If there is no significant difference, then an expanding private sector would not result in an "adverse" selection problem for the public system. Even if there exists some difference in ability, regulation of private-sector prices may limit the incentives for many of the "high quality" doctors to leave the public system or devote more time to their private practice. That is, price regulation of private sector providers is an instrument that governments can use to influence the size and scope of the private sector.

6.3 GENERAL REGULATORY ISSUES TO BE ADDRESSED

(a) Issues Regarding Entry

Much of the debate surrounding the role of the private sector in healthcare involves the issue of what is to be expected when private sector healthcare firms enter a healthcare market currently the sole responsibility of the public sector.

There is some disagreement about the short-run effect of allowing private-sector entry in a formerly publicly-dominated healthcare industry. It is helpful in this regard to consider another service which has a large public-sector presence, education. It is clear that the private sector and the public sector have coexisted in the provision of education for quite sometime in all OECD countries. This has occurred despite the fact that in most countries, publicly-provided education is highly subsidized, which would appear to give the public sector a sizable advantage. The important questions are 1) what contributes to this coexistence? and 2) are consumers and society in general better off with this coexistence?

A key issue arises if the individuals who leave the public system were subsidizing the costs of other individuals. If their contribution to the public system goes with them when they opt out, and they were net contributors to the public system, the cost of healthcare for the remaining members would increase. This would be less of a problem if the tax payments were not transferable, but then another issue would arise: whether public support for the publicly-funded system would be eroded over time. That is, as an increasing number of individuals feel that they do not receive much benefit from the public system, they may decide to reduce their political support for it. If their doing so puts pressure on the politicians to lower the amount or quality of publicly-provided healthcare, then this may result in a lower quality public system. The key point here is the commitment to the public system. As that commitment is stronger, this problem becomes less important. To the extent that the community supports redistribution, any change in the delivery or financing of healthcare to include a larger private role may not lead to adverse effects on the public sector's ability to provide healthcare for low income individuals.

There is also an issue related to the long run effects of private sector entry. Suppose the entry of private healthcare firms results in more individuals using the private system, rather than the publicly funded public system. If the taxes paid by the individual were transferred from the public sector to the private sector, this would certainly have the effect of shrinking the size of the public sector. It would have lower funds, but also lower responsibilities.

(b) Service Obligations of Private Firms

It is clear that the service obligations of a regulated firm (or a healthcare system) can be characterized in a number of ways. One type of obligation is "universal service", as, for example, requirement placed on a private firm (think telephone service) to supply everyone in an area. Laffont and Tirole (2000) cite a definition of universal service obligations given by the Federal Communications Commission when applied to telecommunications as "ensuring quality telecommunications services at affordable rates to consumers, including low income consumers, in all regions of the nation, including rural, insular, and high-cost areas."[263]

Applied to healthcare this concept means that all citizens must be covered by the health-insurance system. It is clear that a major issue in the delivery of healthcare is the issue of equal access to quality care. A corresponding modification to universal service provision might be termed "universal and identical service", which means that not only that all citizens in an area must be covered but the services provided must be identical. It should be noted that this is a much stronger requirement than exists for other regulated industries. The issues here are equivalent care and affordable rates. The obligation of private firms providing telecommunications services, for example, can be interpreted as meaning that some reasonable level of service must be provided at a reasonable rate. In public healthcare systems, the obligation of providers might be termed "high quality healthcare" with limited or no user costs to patients.

The issue of whether consumers are in fact getting equivalent service already exists, particularly in Social Welfare-based systems, where rural residents often complain about an inadequate access to healthcare in their area. Where access to care is lower for rural citizens, then the universal and identical service obligation is not being met. Moreover, in cases where the income taxes paid by rural and urban residents are roughly equal, but access to healthcare differs, cross subsidies for healthcare may be going from rural to urban residents. The point is that existing public healthcare systems fall considerably short in providing universal and identical access to healthcare.

(c) Monitoring the Private Sector

The issue of expenditure control is crucial for both private and public insurance. Private insurance firms must monitor the payouts to providers in order to keep premiums competitive and provide a return to shareholders. Public insurers often regulate healthcare spending by imposing direct expenditure controls, or total payouts to providers. These come in a number of forms. First, there is overall spending control, with hard caps on payments from the public insurer to healthcare providers. Second, there is a delisting of covered health services; that is, transferring some healthcare expenditures to the private sector. Third, there is direct regulation of physician payments, or limitations on the number and use of medical procedures. This approach would be favoured by individuals who feel the General Practitioner does not have sufficient incentives to control the behaviour of specialists, who may recommend expensive medical tests or procedures that may not be justified on health grounds.

(d) HMO's and Managed Care

The United States in recent years has seen an increase in the use of managed care. Whereas only one-quarter of the privately insured population was in managed care in 1987, more than three-quarters are enrolled in managed care today.[264] Managed care means an integration of two former separate industries, medical services and insurance, in the provision of healthcare. In managed care contracts, "insurers commonly use financial incentives to physicians to limit utilization, restrict the services that they provide through command-and-control methods and bargain with provider networks to obtain lower prices."[265] Thus, a Social Welfare-based health system might be described as a monopoly HMO (Health Maintenance Organization).[266]

As Cutler et al. (1998:41) point out, traditional indemnity insurance involves almost no limits on qualified providers, patient choice of providers, or fee-for-service payment of providers with moderate cost sharing. The role of the insurer is limited to paying bills. Managed care, in contrast, involves some restriction on the use of providers, use of either capitation, salary or discounted fee for service, differential cost sharing depending on whether a network of providers is used, with insurers paying bills, forming networks, monitoring utilization, or even providing care. Limits on utilization are almost entirely on the supply side.[267]

Public healthcare systems, much like their private-sector counterparts, face the same issues regarding the effect of the form of physician compensation on physician performance. It has been argued that there are four important dimensions of physician practice that must be considered when one discusses the form of physician compensation. Robinson (2001) suggests the compensation scheme must provide incentives for physicians to 1) increase their productivity and patient service, 2) accept patients with difficult to treat medical conditions, 3) provide the appropriate level of care, and 4) adopt evidence-based best practices.[268] In comparing fee-for-service versus capitation – the payment of a fixed fee per patient per time period – Robinson argues that fee-for-service provides good incentives on criteria 1) and 2) while capitation works well for conditions 3) and 4). Regarding salary as a form of compensation, Robinson argues that "salary undermines productivity, condones on-the-job leisure, and fosters a bureaucratic mentality in which every procedure is someone else's problem."[269] Robinson argues that the peer-reviewed literature generally finds that fee-for-service compensation encourages and capitation discourages the use of medical resources, while productivity-based compensation – like fee for service – encourages, while salary discourages productivity.[270] Robinson concludes that given the limitations of these compensation schemes, the trend for physician payment at least in the U.S. has been to use "blended methods" which attempt to combine elements of the different compensation schemes.[271]

(e) The Issue of Crowding Out

Healthcare observers are concerned with the effect that the coexistence of a private and a public healthcare system has on the long-term stability of the two sectors. In the U.S., the issue is whether the existence and expansion of Medicaid in the 1980s and 1990s – the public insurance program for low-income persons – crowded out the private healthcare system. That is, did the availability of a public alternative lead to a reduction in the purchase of private health insurance? Estimates obtained by Cutler and Gruber (1996) find that approximately 50% of the increase in Medicaid coverage was associated with a reduction in private insurance coverage. They argue that this occurred largely because employees in the U.S. took up employer-based insurance less frequently.

One can also envision a reverse "crowding out" effect which occurs when the existence of private health alternatives reduces the supply of publicly-provided health services. One issue is "whether private financing erodes public support for maintaining healthcare budgets in the public sector."[272] For example, Propper (2000) suggests one possible effect of the growth of the private healthcare sector is that "an increase in the use of private services may be accompanied by a decrease in the support for, and willingness to pay, taxes for the public sector. High private usage leading to lack of 'voice' and taxpayer discontent could lead to the evolution of the NHS into a 'poor service for the poor'".[273] However, Propper argues that this result is less likely if individuals who use private services continue to access the NHS at the same time, and if the use of each sector is not linked. Similarly, Saltman and Von Otter (1992) fear that an expansion of the private sector may force public providers to mimic the profit-oriented strategies of the private sector, and ultimately end the public consensus on the importance of universal publicly- provided health services.[274]

However, it has been suggested the crowding-out effect may operate in quite the opposite fashion. Globerman and Vining (1998) argue that it is possible that government attempts to suppress the growth of private financing may lead to a reduction in nominal public healthcare budgets.[275] For example, if the suppression of private financing results in waiting and related costs becoming sufficiently onerous, a significant number of poorer individuals – which could include middle-income voters – may join a coalition of wealthier individuals to lobby for lower government healthcare taxes in order to fund private-financing options. In other words, the general pattern of having some healthcare cost financed privately, implies that this "safety value" is required to maintain a predominantly public healthcare system.[276]

CHAPTER VII

MODELS OF PARALLEL PUBLIC AND PRIVATE HEALTHCARE SYSTEMS[277]

There are a number of ways in which one can imagine a public and private healthcare system coexisting. However, the key distinction is whether the two systems provide complementary or substitute services. Complementary services are those which the consumer consumes jointly, for example, medical treatment plus a single-person hospital room. It is common for these complementary services to be provided either by the principal health insurer as an option, for example in Belgium, or by a private insurer as in Canada.

For cases where the public system and the private system provide the same type of medical services, it is important to consider how consumers view the separate services provided by the two sectors.[278] One possibility is that the services are viewed as horizontally differentiated, two versions of essentially the same service. For example, consider education. Suppose the quality of education – as determined by the quality of the teachers, resources available, student abilities – is equal between two schools, but they are differentiated in some other dimension, for example, they might be different religious-based schools. In this setting, consumers in aggregate who decide to choose a religious-based education would divide themselves between these two options. Also, if education is horizontally differentiated, then it is possible for higher-cost schools to coexist with lower-cost schools, for example, public schools, even though the education "quality" may be similar. We can term competition of this sort competition between different varieties.

In contrast to the above, suppose the respective services – education in this case – provided by schools is of different qualities. Services in this sense are vertically differentiated. In this case, the only way a higher-cost school can coexist with a lower cost school, is if it provides a higher quality of service. We can term competition in a vertical sense competition between different qualities. Both of these cases are discussed in turn.

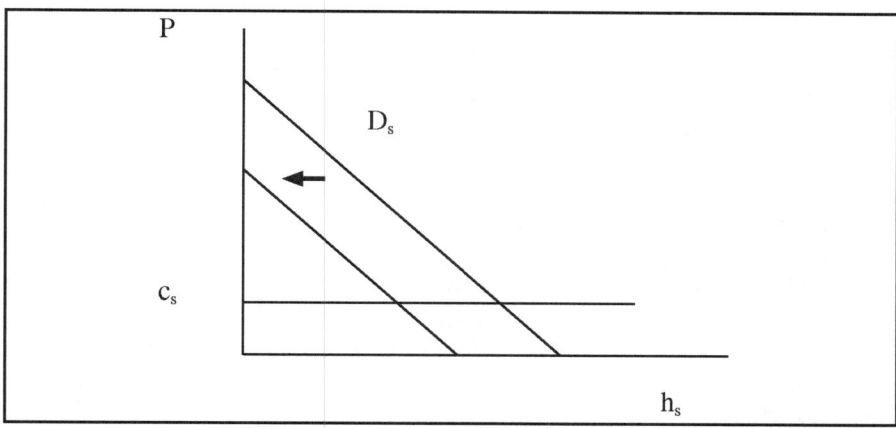

Figure 5: Differentiation by Variety

7.1 COMPETITION BETWEEN FIRMS PROVIDING DIFFERENT VARIETIES

It is possible to consider an important issue that has been raised regarding the coexistence of a public and private sector providing healthcare. For example, it has been argued in the UK that the private sector plays a complementary and important role in supporting the public system, specifically, "by not taking up a place in the NHS queue, they allow the next patient in time to benefit from earlier treatment."[279] This is the role the private sector performs in alleviating the demands on the public system.

Figure 5 illustrates this point. We have two inverse demand curves for the public health service, h_s. The inverse demand curve for public health services with a private healthcare sector is given as $p = a - b\,h_s - c h_p$. Given this demand curve, higher levels of private healthcare services, h_p, lower the demand for the public health services according to the sign and size of the parameter c. If c is positive this means the public and private health services are substitutes, with the degree of substitution measured by the value of c. Larger values of c imply a greater degree of substitution between the two health services and hence larger reduction in demand for the public health services for any given level of private health services. As can be seen, the lower demand curve intersects the marginal cost curve at a lower quantity of public healthcare services, and hence lower total costs incurred by the public sector. It is important to note that if c was negative, then the public and private services would be complements, and the introduction of a private sector would *increase* the demand for the public service, and hence increase its costs. Diagramatically, the demand curve facing the public sector would shift to the right.

The above inverse demand function, it should be noted, comes from an overall market demand that values variety. This would occur if consumers in the aggregate view healthcare provided by the public and private sectors as basically two varieties of the same good, much like education of the same quality provided by two religious-based schools. An important implication of this model is that even with different prices for the public and private service (which are essentially the same quality) then it is possible that the higher priced alternative would still be purchased by some consumers. For example, one sees different tuition levels for different private schools.

7.2 COMPETITION BETWEEN FIRMS PROVIDING DIFFERENT QUALITIES

The issue of competition between firms providing different qualities can be illustrated in the following diagram. Figure 6 illustrates a model of competition between three quality levels of healthcare, for example one might consider three expected quality levels of surgery. The solid lines are labeled $U(y, q_i)$ where q_i, $i = h, m, l$, are the respective qualities, high, medium, and low, and U is the utility level obtained by a consumer with income y who purchases a service of quality q_i.

A useful form for the utility or preference ranking function $U(y,q_i)$ is $U = q_i(y - p_i) = -q_i p_i + q_i y$, which is utility level received from the quality q_i for a price p_i as a function of an individual's income, y. The function reflects the preferences of individuals needing surgery. If all consumers agree on the above ranking, and more importantly, higher income individuals are willing to pay more for higher quality, then the ranking or utility functions are steeper as the quality provided increases. In this model, the intersection of two solid lines indicates the income level at which the two quality-price combinations are considered equivalent. For example, it indicates the income level of an individual who is indifferent between the lower price, lower quality service, and the higher price, higher quality service that is available. The income level y_1^* is the level where an individual considers the lowest quality (and lowest price) equivalent to the medium quality (and medium price). Mathematically

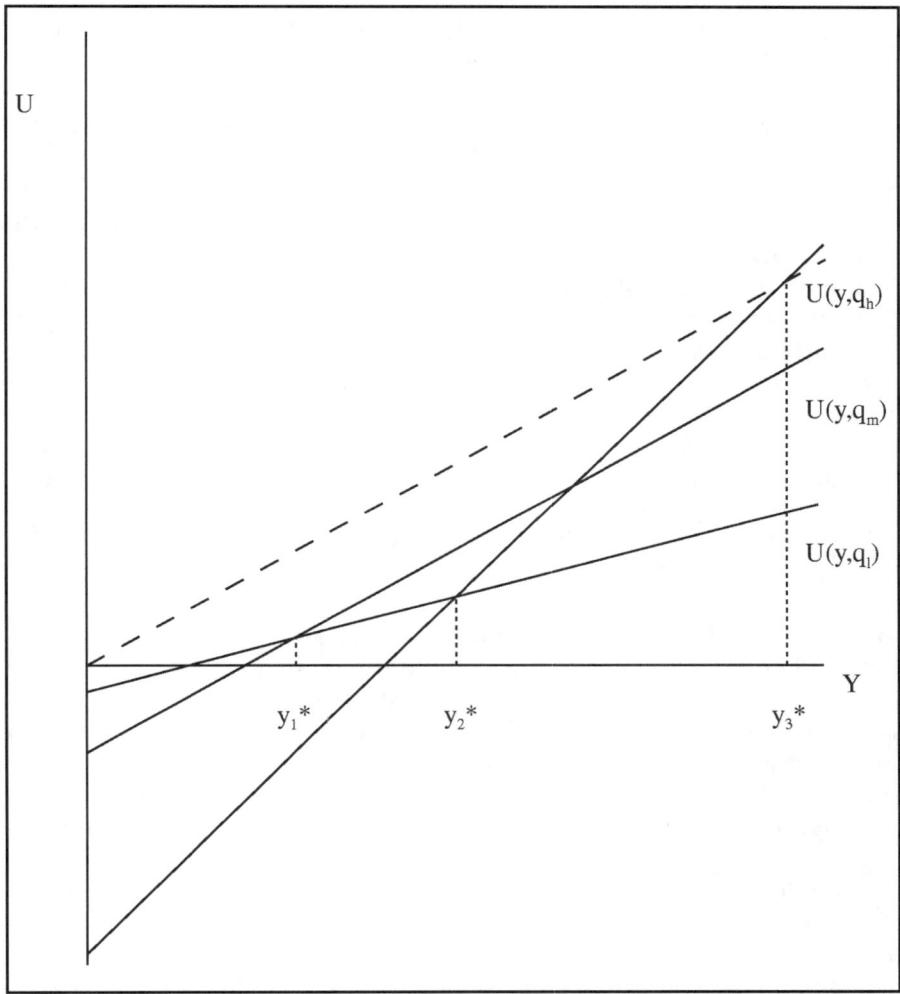

Figure 6: Differentiation by Quality

$U(y,q_l) = U(y,q_m)$ or $-q_l p_l + q_l y = -q_m p_m + q_m y$ or $y_1^* = (q_m p_m - q_l p_l)/(q_m - q_l)$, with a similar approach used to determine y_2^* and y_3^*.

Now we are in a position to use the model. Without government supply of the good, we have three quality levels provided in equilibrium in this model. High-income individuals with incomes above y_2^* purchase the highest quality service; individuals within the income range y_1^* purchase the medium quality range, and individuals within the range

(y_1^*-y_0^*) purchase the lowest quality range. Individuals with incomes below y_0^* do not purchase the good.

Now suppose the government provides a medium quality service at a zero price, financed out of general revenues. This option is depicted on the diagram as the dotted line which indicates the medium quality service is being provided at a zero price. This would be the case if the service was provided at a zero user price or no copayment by the government. The solid curves will shift somewhat now since the income y is after tax income, but the main point can be made using the existing curves. With the introduction of the medium quality service by the government at a zero price, all quality levels below q_m disappear. Note, however, that there remains the possibility for the high quality service to exist. To summarize, the lower the quality of the government supplied service, the lower is the income level at which higher-income individuals prefer the higher quality service. An equilibrium, with a lower quality level provided by the government and a higher quality level provided by the private sector, might be termed a two-tier system.

What is important about the above analysis? First, it is extremely difficult and costly to completely eliminate the demand for higher quality service, in this case health service, if consumers view healthcare in quality terms, and higher income individuals have a higher willingness to pay for quality than lower income individuals. Second, as the perceived quality of the government service declines, the income range at which the high quality sector is preferred increases. That is, only by prohibiting entry, or by raising the quality of care, can the public sector reduce the fraction of people opting for higher quality (actual or perceived) private care.

There is some evidence that the demand for private health insurance is determined by the perceived quality gap between the public and private healthcare systems. Using a data set for Catalonia in Spain, Costa and Garcia (2003) investigate the influence of the quality gap between an NHS type, public system, and private healthcare in combination with the insurance premium, on the demand for voluntary private health insurance. They define a "quality gap" as a result of the uniformity of care and access barriers that characterize NHS-type systems. The uniformity of care may result in a lack of personalized healthcare and a reduction in choice. Costa and Garcia (2003) define access barriers as inpatient and outpatient waiting lists, excessive bureaucracy, unnecessary delays and the need to obtain GP referrals for visits to specialists.

They find that the quality gap in the Spanish healthcare system explains the demand for private health insurance and that an increase in perceived NHS quality is equivalent to a reduction by the same amount in the perceived quality of private healthcare.[280] Similarly, Besley et al (1999), in their examination of the UK health system, found that a key determinant of private insurance demand is the length of long-term waiting lists. In addition, Besley et al (1998) found that in regions with many individuals privately insured, there appears to be fewer resources put into keeping waiting lists short. This is consistent with their view that when individuals opt out of the public system, there is less pressure on healthcare officials to keep waiting lists down.

Presumably, if the care is differentiated not by variety but quality, then the individuals opting out will have a higher quality of care than those remaining. However, it should be noted that education exhibits both differences in quality and differences in variety. The important point raised by the previous analysis is that the results which occur with private education may not be entirely representative of the nature of the competition which would exist between a private and public healthcare sector. To the extent that consumers value differences in quality, the entry of private firms will be found at the high end of the market. The concern then about the existence of a private sector is really about the respective mix of patients remaining, and hence the quality of the care in the two systems.

7.3 DISCUSSION

Hurley et al (2002) examined the Australian experience with parallel finance for inpatient hospital services and argue that "the Australian experience provides a cautionary tale regarding the risks, costs and benefits of a parallel private system of healthcare finance."[281] Hurley et al argue that the private parallel system in Australia has not had a significant effect on the costs of the public hospital system for a number of reasons. First, they argue the subsidy provided for the purchase of health insurance (30% subsidy) has resulted not in a net increase in private financing but merely a switch from self-insuring (paying out of pocket) to private insurance coverage.[282] In addition, the subsidy led to a slight increase in private insurance purchases by young Australians (which is desirable under the lifetime coverage provision) who are relatively healthy and hence are not major users of the public hospital system. Second, they argue that in the Australian case the private and public health sectors were not truly separate, it that the privately insured services often generated additional costs for the public sector – privately financed surgery generating pre and post-op public health visits – and the increased demand for healthcare inputs overall increased the costs of providing public health services.[283]

7.4 EMPIRICAL EVIDENCE – FOR PROFIT VERSUS NOT FOR PROFIT HOSPITAL CARE

The issue of the respective performance of the for-profit versus not-for-profit sectors in the delivery of healthcare has resulted in an increasing amount of research activity. In a comprehensive analysis of this literature, Currie, Donaldson and Lu (2003) examined thirty-four studies that examined this issue and reported that most of the studies found no difference between for-profit and not-for-profit full-service hospitals with respect to relative costs, quality of care or efficiency.[284] Regarding the issue of quality differences between for-profit and not-for-profit hospitals, they find that there are few studies of this issue, because of the difficulty in measuring "quality" in hospital settings. Of eleven studies, seven were not able to make a clear conclusion and the remaining four showed a slight quality difference in favour of not-for-profit hospitals; but even these results can be challenged.[285] Perhaps most importantly, they argue that this research, which is largely based on U.S. studies of for-profit versus not-for-profit care, has little relevance to the issue of contracting out of surgical services by health authorities, which was the focus of Alberta's *Healthcare Protection Act* of 1999. They point out that there is "no published evidence on the specific question of health authorities contracting-out surgical services to private providers."[286]

CHAPTER VIII

CONCLUSION

This study has examined the role of the private sector in a number of OECD countries. While all systems share a commitment to universal coverage, there is a remarkable variation in the role assigned to the private sector. The role ranges from private supplementary insurance to private hospitals and clinics providing services to the public sector.

A common theme is that the role of the private sector is now too important to eliminate, even in the U.K., which has embarked on a massive increase in funding for the private sector. According to the authors of the most recent healthcare plan in Britain, "ideological boundaries or institutional barriers should not stand in the way of better care for NHS patients. ... The private and voluntary sectors have a role to play in ensuring that NHS patients get the full benefit from this extra investment. By constructing the right partnerships the NHS can harness the capacity of private and voluntary providers to treat more NHS patients."

It seems clear that once a commitment is made to provide healthcare coverage to all citizens, a great variety of private-sector involvement can be integrated into largely publicly-provided healthcare systems. Overall, the Social Insurance-based healthcare systems, like Germany, France and Belgium, have been successful in providing high quality universal service while allowing a significant role for the private sector. These systems, in contrast to the Social Welfare systems of the UK, Sweden and Australia, also feature an arm's length insurer or insurers who have considerable autonomy from government. In appears that an advantage of Social Insurance-based systems is that every healthcare decision does not become a political issue. The Social Insurance-based systems seem to be able to meet the expectations of their clientele while maintaining a strong commitment to social solidarity. The German system allows higher income individuals to opt out of the public system and yet the public system still provides a high level of service to those who remain.

Even with the Social Welfare systems there seems to be a consensus developing that the traditional command-and-control system of healthcare provision has its limitations. A recognition that markets and incentives can improve performance within the area of healthcare is developing. From an examination of the U.K., Swedish and Australian systems, it appears that the most promising role for the private sector is to provide a range of elective surgeries based on contracts with the public insurer. Elective surgeries seem to be the area generating the most dissatisfaction within these systems, and this area of the healthcare system seems to offer the potential for efficiency gains through regulation. It also appears that it is quite difficult to replicate the benefits of a competitive healthcare system within a publicly managed and financed healthcare system like the U.K. A major problem plaguing Social Welfare based systems is that public provision obscures the cost of providing the different types of medical services. Experiments with private-sector provision subject to government regulation may allow more efficient forms of healthcare provision to arise.

The countries examined here all share a commitment to ensuring adequate healthcare for all its citizens. This commitment has being maintained while still permitting a range of consumer choice and private-sector involvement. It is hoped that the issues raised in this study can inform debate in Canada regarding the options and possibilities for revitalizing the nation's healthcare system.

REFERENCES

Aaron, Henry J. (2003) "The Costs of Health Care Administration in the United States and Canada – Questionable Answers to a Questionable Question" *New England Journal of Medicine*, 349, 8, 801-803.

Aris, Ben (2003) "Commission recommends reform of German health care" *The Lancet*, 362, 1388.

Altenstetter, Christa (2003) "Insights From Health Care in Germany" *American Journal of Public Health*, 93, 38-44.

Anell, Anders (1996) "The monopolistic integrated model and health care reform: the Swedish experience" *Health Policy*, 37, 19-33.

Arrow, K.J. (1963) "Uncertainty and the Welfare Economics of Medical Care" *American Economic Review*, December.

Australian Institute of Health & Welfare (AIHW). Australian's Health 2000. Canberra:AIHW. Melbourne: Oxford University Press.

Bach, Stephen (1994) "Managing a Pluralist Health System: The Case of Health Care Reform in France" *International Journal of Health Services*, 24, 593-606.

Baumol, William J. (1993) "Health care, education and the cost disease: a looming crisis for public choice" *Public Choice*, 77, 17-28.

Besley, Timothy, John Hall and Ian Preston (1998) "Private and public health insurance in the UK" *European Economic Review*, 42, 491-497.

Besley, T. John Hall and Ian Preston (1996) "The demand for private health insurance: do waiting lists matter?" *Journal of Public Economics*, 72, 155-181.

Besley, T. and S. Coate (1991) "Public Provision of private goods and the redistribution of income" *American Economic Review*, 81, 979-984.

Birchard, Karen (2003) "German health reform expected by month's end" *Medical Post*, January 14, 2003.

Bishai, David M. and Hui Chu Lang (2000) "The willingness to pay for wait reduction: the disutility of queues for cataract surgery in Canada, Denmark and Spain" *Journal of Health Economics*, 19, 219-230.

Blomqvist, Å.G. and R.A.L. Carter (1997) "Is health care really a luxury" *Journal of Health Economics*, 16, 207-209.

Boadway, Robin W. and David E. Wildasin *Public Sector Economics*, Second Edition, Boston: Little, Brown and Company, 1984.

Boadway, Robin (1997) "Presidential Address: Public economics and the theory of public policy" *Canadian Journal of Economics*, 30, 753-772.

British Medical Association, *Changing the Contractual Status of Consultants*, Health policy and economic research unit – Discussion paper 7, May 2001a.

British Medical Association, *Briefing Notes* – Doctors Pay, 2001b.

Busse Reinhard (1999) "Priority-setting and rationing in German Health care" *Health Policy*, 50, 71-90.

Calnan, Michael. Sarah Cant and Jonathan Gabe *Going Private: Why People Pay for Their Health Care*, Buckingham: Open University Press, 1993.

Costa, Joan and Jaume García (2003) "Demand for private health insurance: how important is the quality gap?" *Health Economics*, 12, 587-599.

Chase, Chevy (1998) "Why Britain is reorganizing its national health service – yet again" *Health Affairs*, 17, 11-125.

Culyer, A.J. (1989) "The Normative Economics of Health Care Finance and Provision" *Oxford Review of Economic Policy*, 5, 34-58.

Competitive Health Care in Europe: Future Prospects, Edited by A.F. Casparie, H.E.G.M. Hermans and J.H.P. Paelinck, Aldershot: Dartmouth, 1990.

Cullis, J.G. and P.R. Jones (1985) "National Health Service Waiting Lists: A Discussion of Competing Explanations and a Policy Proposal" *Journal of Health Economics*, 4, 119-135.

Cullis, J.G. and P.R. Jones (1986) "Rationing by waiting lists: an implication" *American Economic Review*, 76, 250-256.

Cullis, John G., Philip R. Jones and Carol Propper "Waiting Lists and Medical Treatment: Analysis and Policies" in *Handbook of Health Economics*, Volume 1B, Amsterdam: New York and Oxford, Elsevier Science, North Holland, 2000.

Currie, Gillian, Cam Donaldson and Mingshan Lu (2003) "What Does Canada Profit from the For-Profit Debate on Health Care?" *Canadian Public Policy*, 29, 2, 227-251.

Cutler, David M., Mark McClellan and Joseph P. Newhouse "Prices and Productivity in Managed Care Insurance" Working Paper 6677, Cambridge, National Bureau of Economic Research, Inc. August 1998.

Culyer, A.J. (1989) "The Normative Economics of Health Care Finance and Provision" *Oxford Review of Economic Policy*, 5, 34-58.

Davoren, Peter (2001) "Why private health insurance initiatives don't help public hospitals" *New Doctor*, 75, Winter 2001, 1-5.

De Graeve, Diana, Ilse Janssens, and Hilde Meersman (1998) "Fee Determination in the Belgian Health Care Market" *Journal d'Economie Médicale*, 16, 39-50.

Demsetz, Harold (1968) "Why Regulate Utilities?" *Journal of Law and Economics*, April 1968.

Diderichsen, Finn (1999) "Devolution in Swedish Health Care: Local government isn't powerful enough to control costs or stop privatisation" *British Medical Journal*, 318, 1156-1157.

Diderichsen, Finn (1995) "Market Reforms in health care and sustainability of the welfare state: lessons from Sweden" *Health Policy*, 32, 141-153.

Donaldson, L.J., Maratos, J.I. and R.A. Richardson (1984) "A Review of an Orthopaedic In-Patient Waiting List" *Health Trends*, February, 14-5.

Doyal, Len and Lesley Doyal (1999) "The British National Health Service: A Tarnished Moral Vision? *Health Care Analysis*, 7, 363-376.

Doyle, Yvonne and Adrian Bull (2000) "Role of the Private Sector in the United Kingdom healthcare system" *British Medical Journal*, 321, 563-565.

Dranove, David (1998) "Economies of scale in non-revenue producing cost centers: implications for hospital mergers" *Journal of Health Economics*, 17, 69-83.

Dunn, Daniel L., et al. (1995) "Economies of Scope in Physicians' Work: The Performance of Multiple Surgery," *Inquiry*, 32, 87-101.

Economist.com (2003) *Reviving the sick men of Europe*, London: July 24, 2003, p.1.

Enthoven, Alain C. (2000) "In Pursuit of an Improving National Health Service" *Health Affairs*, 19, 102-119.

Enthoven, A. (1986) "Managed Competition in health care and the unfinished agenda" *Health Care Financing Review*, annual supplement, 105-119.

Enthoven, A. *Reflections on the Management of the National Health Service*, London, Nuffield Provincial Hospitals' Trust, 1985.

Epple, D. and R. Romano (1996) "Public Provision of private goods" *Journal of Political Economy*, 104, 57-84.

European Observatory on Health Care Systems, *Health Care Systems in Transition* – Belgium, 2000.

European Observatory on Health Care Systems, *Health Care Systems in Transition* – United Kingdon, 1999.

European Observatory on Health Care Systems, *Health Care Systems in Transition* – Sweden, 2001

European Observatory on Health Care Systems, *Health Care Systems in Transition* – Germany, 2000.

Evans, R.G. *Strained Mercy: The Economics of Canadian Health Care*, Toronto: Butterworth, 1984.

Farnworth, Michael G. (2003) "A game theoretic model of the relationship between prices and waiting times" *Journal of Health Economics*, 22, 47-60.

Ferris, J. Stephen and Edwin G. West (1996) "The cost disease and government growth: Qualifications to Baumol" *Public Choice*, 89, 35-52.

Fielding, Jonathan E. and Pierre-Jean Lancry (1993) "Lessons from France – 'Vive la Différence': The French Health Care System and US Health System Reform" *JAMA*, 270, 748-756.

Folland, Sherman, Allen C. Goodman, and Miron Stano *The Economics of Health and Health Care*, Upper Saddle River, Prentice-Hall, 2001.

Fourier, Gary M. and Jean M. Mitchell, (1992) "Hospital Costs and Competition for Services: A Multiproduct Analysis," *Review of Economics and Statistics*, 74, 627-634.

Gabel, Jon, Steven DiCarlo, Steven Fink, and Gregory de Lissovoy, "Employer-Sponsored Health Insurance in America" *Health Affairs*, 8(2), 1989, 116-128.

Garpenby, Peter (1995) "Health Care Reform in Sweden in the 1990s: Local Pluralism versus National Coordination" *Journal of Health Politics, Policy and Law*, 20, 695-717.

Globerman, Steven and Aidan Vining (1998) "A Policy Perspective on "Mixed" Health Care Financial Systems of Business and Economics" *The Journal of Risk and Insurance*, 65, 57-80.

Gouveia, M. (1996) "Majority rule and the public provision of health care" *Public Choice*, 93, 221-244.

Gratzer, David *Code Blue: Revising Canada's Healthcare System*, ECW Press 1999

Gravelle, Hugh, Mark Dusheiko and Matthew Sutton (2002) "The demand for elective surgery in a public system: time and money prices in the UK National Health Service" *Journal of Health Economics*, 21, 423-449.

Gray, Gwen (1998) "Access to Medical Care under Strain: New Pressures in Canada and Australia" 6, 912.

Grytten, Jostein and Rune Sørenson (2001) "Type of contract and supplier-induced demand for primary physicians in Norway" *Journal of Health Economics*, 20, 379-393.

Hall, J. Incremental Change in the Australia Health Care System, *Health Affairs*. May/June 1999, volume 18, No 3, pg.95-110.

Hall, Jane, Richard De Abreu Lourenco and Rosalie Viney (1999) "Carrots and Sticks – The Fall and Fall of Private Health Insurance in Australia" *Health Economics*, 8, 653-660.

Ham, Chris (1998) "Retracing the Oregon trail: the experience of rationing and the Oregon health plan" *British Medical Journal*, 316, 1-7.

Harrison, Michael I. And Johan Calltorp (2000) "The reorientation of market-oriented reforms in Swedish health care" *Health Policy*, 50, 219-240.

Hoel, Michael and Erik Magnus Saether (2003) "Public health care with waiting time: the role of supplementary private health care" *Journal of Health Economics*, 22, 599-616.

Hopkins, Sandra and H.E. Frech III (2001) "The Rise of Private Health Insurance in Australia: Early Effects on Insurance and Hospital Markets" *The Economic and Labour Relations Review*, 12, 225-238.

Howe,A.. The economics of aged care: achieiving quality and containing costs in Mooney, G.and R. Scotton (eds) 1999. *Economics and Australian Health Policy*. New South Wales: Allen and Unwin.

Hudson, Bob (1999) "Decentralization and Primary Care Groups: a paradigm shift for the National Health Service in England" *Policy & Politics*, 27, 2, 159-172.

Hurley, Jeremiah, Rhema Vaithianathan, Thomas F. Crossley, and Deborah Cobb-Clark "Parallel Private Health Insurance in Australia: A Cautionary Tale and Lessons for Canada" Institute for the Study of Labour, IZA DP No. 515, June 2002.

Internal Markets in the Making: Health Systems in Canada, Iceland and the United Kingdom, Health Policy Studies No. 6, Paris: Organisation for Economic Co-operation and Development, 1995.

Ireland, Norman J. Ireland (1990) "The Mix of Social and Private Provision of Goods and Services" *Journal of Public Economics*, 43, 201-219.

Iversen, Tor (1997) "The effect of a private sector on the waiting time in a national health service" *Journal of Health Economics*, 16, 381-396.

Jensen, Gail A., Michael A. Morrisey, Shannon Gaffney, and Derek K. Liston, "The New Dominance of Managed Care: Insurance Trends in the 1990s" *Health Affairs*, January/February 1997, 16(1), 125-136.

Jofre-Bonet, Mireia (2000) "Public health care and private insurance demand: The waiting time as a link, " *Health Care Management Science*, 3, 51-71.

Kamke, Kerstin (1998) "The German health care system and health care reform" *Health Policy*, 43, 171-194.

Karcher, Helmut (1996) "German health insurance system faces new deficits" *British Medical Journal*, 312, 74-75.

Karcher, Helmut (1997) "Germany's new health reforms" *British Medical Journal*, 314, 845.

Keen, Justin (2000) "Commentary: Cooperation should be based on what the public wants and needs from its healthcare system" *British Medical Journal*, 321, 563.

King, Derek and Alan Maynard (1999) "Public Opinion and rationing in the United Kingdom" *Health Policy*, 50, 39-53.

Kloiber, Otmar and Verena Hoppe (2001) *The German Health Care System: A Brief Introduction*, German Medical Association, mimeo.

Laffont, Jean-Jacques and Jean Tirole , *Competition in Telecommunications*, Cambridge: MIT Press, 2000.

Lancry, Pierre-Jean and Simone Sandier (1999) "Rationing health care in France" *Health Policy*, 50, 23-38.

LeGrand, J., N. Mays and J. Mulligan, *Learning from the NHS Internal Market*, London: King's Fund, 1998.

Lewis, MJ. and Leeder, SR. *Where to from here? The need to construct a comprehensive national health care policy*. Australian Health Policy Institute Commissioned Paper Series 20001/01.

Limits to Care: Reforming Canada's Health System in an Age of Restraint, Åke Blomqvist and David M.. Brown editors, Toronto: C.D. Howe Institute, 1994.

Lindsay, C.M. and B. Feigenbaum (1984) "Rationing by waiting lists" *American Economic Review*, 74, 404-417.

Locock, Louise (2000) "The Changing Nature of Rationing in the UK National Health Service" *Public Administration*, 78, 91-109.

Martin, Stephen and Peter C. Smith (1999) "Rationing by waiting lists: an empirical investigation" *Journal of Public Economics*, 71, 141-164.

Mooney G. Health Economics and Health Policy in Mooney, G. and Scotton R.(eds) *Economics and Australian Health Policy*. New South Wales: Allen and Unwin., 1999.

Nicholson, Bryan (1998) "Private care eases public burden" *Management Today*; London, Aug 1998, 1-2.

Nolte, Ellen and Martin McKee (2000) "Ten Years of German Unification" *British Medical Journal*, 321, 1094-1095.

Nonneman, W.L.M. "Health Care in Belgium" in *Competitive Health Care in Europe: Future Prospects*, Edited by A.F. Casparie, H.E.G.M. Hermans and J.H.P. Paelinck, Aldershot: Dartmouth, 1990.

Nonneman, Walter and Eddy van Doorslaer (1994) "The Role of the Sickness Funds in the Belgian Health Care Market" *Soc. Sci. Med.*, 39, 1483-1495.

Olivella, Pau (2002) "Shifting public-health-sector waiting lists to the private sector" *European Journal of Political Economy*, 19, 103-132.

Pauly, Mark and John Goodman (1995) "Tax Credits for Health Insurance and Medical Savings Acounts" *Health Affairs*, 14, 1, 126-139.

Private Health Insurance, Occasional Papers, New Series No. 4. *Department of Health and Aged Care*, 2000.

Propper, Carol, Bronwyn Croxson and Arran Shearer (2002) "Waiting times for hospital admissions: the impact of GP fundholding" *Journal of Health Economics*, 21, 227-252.

Propper, Carol (2000) "The demand for private health care in the UK" *Journal of Health Economics*, 19, 855-876.

Propper, Carol (1995) "The Disutility of Time Spent on the United Kingdom's National Health Service Waiting Lists" *The Journal of Human Resources*, 20, 677-701.

Quatreboeufs, Docteur Marie-Françoise *Le Systeme Francais De Protection Sociale*, Paris: Caisse Nationale de l'Assurance Maladie des Travailleurs Salariés, Le 27 Octobre 1999.

Rapport Annuel INAMI 1999, Bruxelles: INAMI, 2000

Robinson, James C. "Theory and Practice in the Design of Physician Payment Incentives" The Milbank Quarterly, 79, 2, 2001.

Rodwin, Victor G. (2003) "The Health Care System Under French National Health Insurance: Lessons for Health Reform in the United States" *American Journal of Public Health*, 93, 31-37.

Rodwin, Victor G. and Simone Sandier (1993) "Health Care Under French National Health Insurance" *Health Affairs*, 12, 11-131.

Rothschild M. and J.E. Stiglitz (1976) "Equilibrium in Competitive Insurance Markets: An Essay in the Economics of Imperfect Information" *Quarterly Journal of Economics*, 80, 629-49.

Salkeld G. Mitchell, A and Hill S. Pharmaceuticals. 1999. E*conomics and Australian Health Policy*. New South Wales: Allen and Unwin.

Saltman. Richard B. and Casten von Otter *Planned Markets and Public Competition: Strategic Reform in Northern European Health Systems*, Buckingham, Open University Press, 1992.

Saltman, Richard B. (1997) "The context for health reform in the United Kingdom, Sweden, Germany, and the United States" *Health Policy*, 41, S9-S26.

Saltman, Richard B. and Josep Figueras (1998) "Analyzing the Evidence on European Health Care Reforms" *Health Affairs*, March/April, 85-108.

Saltman, Richard B. (2003) "Melting public-private boundaries in European health systems" *European Journal of Public Health*, 13, 24-29.

Schokkaert, Erik and Carine Van de Voorde (2003) "Belgium: risk adjustment and financial responsibility in a centralised system" *Health Policy*, 65, 5-19.

Schut, Frederik T. and Eddy K.A. van Doorslaer (1999) "Towards a reinforced agency role of health insurers in Belgium and the Netherlands" *Health Policy*, 48, 47-67.

Sjöberg, Kerstin (2001) "Presentation: The Swedish Health Care System" Federation of Swedish Council Councils.

Stoddart, G. and R. Labelle, *Privatization in the Canadian Health Care System: Assertions, Evidence, Ideology, and Options*, Canada: Ministry of Supply and Services, 1985.

Swedish Institute. The Health Care System in Sweden: Fact Sheets on Sweden. Stockholm: Swedish Institute, May 1999.

The Economist (2003) *Europe: Is it enough?; Germany's health-care reform*, London: June 7, 2003, pg. 36.

Thorpe, Jacqueline (2003) "Germany's 'tectonic' shift on welfare" *National Post*, October 20, 2003.

Tirole, Jean, *The Theory of Industrial Organization*, Cambridge: MIT Press, 1988.

Tobin, James (1994) *"Health care reform as seen by a general economist"* reprinted in James Tobin, *Full Employment and Growth: Further Keynesian Essays on Policy*, Cheltenham: Edward Elgar, 1996.

Tuffs, Annette (2000) "Germany expects more hospital privatisation" *British Medical Journal*, 320, 1030.

The NHS Plan, Presented to Parliament by the Secretary of State for Health By Command of Her Majesty, July 2000.

Viscusi, W. Kip, John M. Vernon and Joseph E. Harrington Jr. *The Economics of Regulation and Antitrust*, Cambridge: MIT Press, 2000.

Wagstaff, Adam (1991) "QALYs and the equity-efficiency trade-off" *Journal of Health Economics*, 10, 21-41.

West, Peter A. (1998) "Market – what market? A review of Health Authority in the NHS internal market" *Health Policy*, 44, 167-183.

Whitehead, Margaret, Rolf Å Gustafsson, and Finn Diderichsen (1997) "Why is Sweden rethinking its NHS style reforms?" *British Medical Journal*, 315: 935-939.

Williamson, Oliver E. (1976) "Franchise Bidding for Natural Monopolies – In General and with Respect to CATV" *Bell Journal of Economics*, 7, 73-104.

Worthington, D. (1987) "Queuing models for hospital waiting lists" *Journal of Operations Research Society*, 38, 413-422.

Y.W. van Kemenade, *Health care in Europe*, National Council for Public Health, 1993.

ENDNOTES

1 See for example the collection of essays in *Limits to Care: Reforming Canada's Health System in an Age of Restraint*, Åke Blomqvist and David M. Brown editors, Toronto: C.D. Howe Institute, 1994. For an earlier examination of the Canadian health care system see Evans (1984).

2 The efficiency standard most often used in economics measures societal welfare (or allocative efficiency) as the sum of consumer and producer surplus. Given constant returns to scale in production, this is equivalent to maximizing consumer surplus which is defined as the difference between the amount that all consumers are willing to pay and the price they are charged. If income effects are small, a downward sloping demand curve can be thought of as ordering the willingness to pay of consumers from highest to lowest with each consumer demanding one unit of care.

3 As an example, suppose the total cost of the accident is $1000, and the probability of an accident is 1/4. The premium that would be charged by a competitive insurance firm, with no insurance provision costs (loading) would be $250.00.

4 For a seminal treatment of the role of information in the provision of insurance when insurers cannot identify the risk categories of individuals, see Rothschild and Stiglitz (1976).

5 Note that insurance is also purchased when the possible costs in the bad state are significantly less than the costs for medical treatment, for example, dental care. Furthermore, insurance is also purchased when treatment (repair) is not as critical as in automobile insurance.

6 Included in this is self-insurance, where the individual saves a certain amount of money in the good states (no illness) to be used in the bad states (illness). A version of this is called Medical Savings Account, which involves an account set up by government to be used by individuals for healthcare expenditures. This may involve the individual being able to realize any savings from lower use of medical services, due to perhaps good fortune, preventative care, or both. Proposed benefits are increased incentives for lower healthcare consumption, which, however, comes at the expense of reduced risk pooling.

7 In reality, the consumer often goes directly to the GP (General Practitioner) – given that most private health insurance contracts provide for a given number of GP visits.

8   What are termed Social Welfare based systems in this study are often called National Insurance Health systems (NIH). The latter term is somewhat misleading because while the health system applies on a national basis, the structure and operation of the health system and corresponding discussion of issues is only loosely based on insurance principles.
9   This is similar to the funding of Employment Insurance and the Canada Pension Plan in Canada.
10 Ministry of Health Services, Government of British Columbia web site (http://www.hlth.gov.bc.ca./msp/infoben/premium.html).
11 Alberta Health Care Insurance Plan, web site, (http://www.health.gov.ab.ca/ahcip/benefits.htm).
12 OECD Health Data 2001.
13 Other definitions of privatization exist. Gray (1998) provides a number of definitions. One definition used in the healthcare literature, attributed to Stoddart and Labelle (1985:1) says "privatization may refer to activities of financing, ownership, management, regulation, or administration – or combinations of these – each with its own and likely different impact on the health care system". A second definition used in the United States views privatization as the practice of the public sector entering into contracts with private agencies for the supply of publicly financed services. Third, privatization may be used in a broad sense to mean the withdrawal of the public responsibility for the financing of services.
14 Saltman (2003:24). Saltman discusses a number of cases where the public/private boundary has been blurred, which will be discussed further in the paper.
15 Saltman (2003:26).
16 Doyal and Doyal (1999:365).
17 OECD (1995:12).
18 Quoted in Chase (1998:115).
19 OECD (1995:12).
20 OECD (1995:13).
21 Saltman and von Otter (1992:22).
22 Alain C. Enthoven (1985:1).
23 Enthoven (1985:2) also states that "competitive tendering from commercial contractors for catering, cleaning, and laundry services could yield significant financial savings. Competitive tendering can be the entering wedge for a great deal of management improvement".
24 Enthoven (1985:13) states that an example of perverse incentives in the structure of the NHS is when " a District that develops an excellent service in some specialty that attracts more referrals is likely to get more work without getting more resources to do it. A District that does a poor job will 'export' patients and have less work, but not correspondingly less resources, for its reward. "

25 Enthoven (1985:26).
26 Department of Health (1998).
27 The European Observatory of Health Systems, *Health Care Systems in Transition – United Kingdom* 1999, p.33.
28 West (1998:168).
29 West (1998:168).
30 TPPs are defined as total purchasing pilots.
31 For a discussion of the role of TPPs as well as a number of issues related to organizational change within the NHS see Hudson (1999).
32 Enthoven (2000:106).
33 *NHS Plan* (2000:10).
34 *NHS Plan* (2000: 5).
35 *NHS Plan* (2000:96).
36 *NHS Plan* (2000:96).
37 *NHS Plan* (2000:96-97), Sections 11.2 and 11.3.
38 Calnan, Cant and Gabe (1993:ix).
39 Doyal and Doyal (1999:364).
40 Saltman (2003:27).
41 European Union of Independent Hospitals (2001:146).
42 A number of criteria are used by the DDRB to determine the appropriate level of compensation for doctors which include (i) affordability, (ii) state of the economy – in particular price inflation, (iii) recruitment, (iv) retention, (v) the nature and volume of workload, (vi) morale and motivation, (vii) job security and findings from studies of pay comparability, and (viii) pensions and other benefits, BMA (2001b:1).
43 It has been estimated that the average consultant works around 50 hours per week on NHS activities, BMA (2001b:6). The flexibility is seen as the result of the pattern of medical work which makes in difficult for consultants to work to a rigid timetable or restrict their hours of work to a given number of set times during the week. Consultants usually have job plans which involve the setting of a fixed number of commitments per week (a minimum of five notionally half days) with the remainder of their workload including regular on-call responsibilities.
44 BMA (2001b:6).
45 Nicholson (1998:1).
46 European Observatory on Health Systems, *United Kingdom*, 1999, p.44.
47 The following data is from Lang and Buisson (1997) *Laing's Healthcare Market Review 1997-1998*, reported in EOHS UK (1999:44).
48 British Medical Association, *Changing the Contractual Status of Consultants*, Health policy and economic research unit – Discussion paper 7, May 2001.
49 BMA (2001:1).

50 BMA (2001:1). The BMA points out that the legal profession in the UK features self-employment while being heavily dependent in its criminal and family forms on public sector finance through legal aid.
51 Rodwin and Sandier (1993:111).
52 Fielding and Lancry (1993:748).
53 Fielding and Lancry (1993:749).
54 Fielding and Lancry (1993:749).
55 Rodwin and Sandier (1993:113).
56 Rodwin and Sandier (1993:113).
57 The following draws heavily from Lancry and Sandier (1999:25-27).
58 Fielding and Lancry (1993:750).
59 Fielding and Lancry (1993:750).
60 The following is based on the Docteur Marie-Françoise Quatreboeufs, *Le Systeme Francais de Protection Sociale*, Caisse Nationale de l'Assurance Maladie des Travailleurs Salariés, 27 Octobre 1999, with translation assistance from Anna Birtles.
61 Quatreboeufs (1999:22).
62 Belgium and Luxembourg also use this system.
63 Rodwin and Sandier (1993:112).
64 Services des Statistiques des Etudes et des Systémes d'Information (SESI). Comptes Nationaux de la Santé 1998. Paris: Ministère de l'Emploi et de la Solidarité, 1998.
65 van Kemenade (1993:39).
66 Rodwin and Sandier (1993:117).
67 Lancry and Sandier (1999:25).
68 Fielding and Lancry (1993:750).
69 Rodwin and Sandier (1993:113).
70 Fielding and Lancry (1993:751).
71 Fielding and Lancry (1993:751).
72 Fielding and Lancry (1993:751).
73 Rodwin and Sandier (1993:114).
74 Rodwin and Sandier (1993:115).
75 The National Qualified Target (OQN) is a regulation governing the financial budgets of the French health system which involves a provisional rate of yearly increases adjusted for volumes (European Union of Independent Hospitals 2001, p.67).
76 The following is drawn from a series of articles from the *British Medical Journal* written by Alexander Dorozynski.
77 A. Dorozynski, *British Medical Journal*, November 25, 1995.
78 A. Dorozynski, *British Medical Journal*, October 5, 1996.
79 A. Dorozynski, *British Medical Journal*, April 5, 1997.

80 A. Dorozynski, *British Medical Journal*, January 9, 1999.
81 A. Dorozynski, *British Medical Journal*, September 27, 1997.
82 A. Dorozynski, *British Medical Journal*, April 4, 1998.
83 The lump sum per suscriber is Fr 150 (£15.50, $24.80) with the agreed fee of Fr 115 (£12) for each visit, A. Dorozynski, *British Medical Journal*, December 5, 1998.
84 A. Dorozynski, *British Medical Journal*, May 9, 1998.
85 A. Dorozynski, *British Medical Journal*, February 5, 2000.
86 A. Dorozynski, *British Medical Journal*, January 6, 1999.
87 A. Dorozynski, *British Medical Journal*, September 2, 2000.
88 Kamke (1998:171).
89 Kloiber and Hoppe (2001:6).
90 Kamke (1998:172).
91 Kamke (1998:172).
92 Kamke (1998:173).
93 Kloiber and Hoppe (2001:8).
94 Kloiber and Hoppe (2001:4).
95 If self-employed individuals have been a member of an SHI at one time, they are not prevented from being an SHI member. Farmers must be members of an SHI. See, EOHCS – Germany (2000:49).
96 EOHCS – Germany (2000:49).
97 EOHCS – Germany (2000:40).
98 See EOHCS – Germany (2000:41) for more details on the compensation scheme.
99 EOHCS – Germany (2000:42).
100 Kamke (1998:173).
101 Kloiber and Hoppe (2001:9).
102 Hinrichs (1995:666).
103 Hinrichs (1995:668).
104 Karcher (1996:74).
105 Karcher (1996:74).
106 Karcher (1997:845).
107 Nolte and McKee (2000:1094).
108 Nolte and McKee (2000:1094).
109 Nolte and McKee (2000:1094).
110 Tuffs (2000:1030).
111 Tuffs (2000:1030).
112 Tuffs (2000:1030
113 Nooneman and van Doorslaer (1994:1483).
114 van Kemenade (1993:27).
115 Nooneman (1990:52).

116 Noonenman and van Doorlslaer (1994:1484). This was as of 1991, latest statistics EOHCS (2000:13) report no change in membership for the Christian and Socialist mutualities.
117 Nooneman (1990:54).
118 EOCHS – Belgium 2000, p.22.
119 For a useful summary see EOHCS – Belgium 2000, p.16.
120 The following is drawn from *Rapport Annuel INAMI 1999*, Bruxelles: INAMI. Translation of relevant passages was done by Anna Birtles.
121 van Kemenade (1993:28).
122 Nooneman (1990).
123 Nooneman (1990:56).
124 Nooneman (1990:56).
125 EOHCS – Belgium 2000, p.26.
126 EOHCS – Belgium 2000, p. 21.
127 Nonneman and van Doorslaer (1994:1484).
128 Nonneman and van Doorslaer (1994:1485).
129 De Graeve et al. (1998:40).
130 De Graeve et al. (1998:41).
131 Nonneman and van Doorslaer (1994:1485).
132 Nonneman and van Doorslaer (1994:1486).
133 EOHCS – Belgium 2000, p.14.
134 EOHCS – Belgium 2000, p. 26.
135 EOHCS – Belgium 2000, p. 15.
136 EOHCS – Belgium 2000, p.15.
137 EOHCS – Belgium 2000, p.72.
138 Ministry for Social Affairs, Public Health and Environment, Belgium.
139 EOHCS – Belgium 2000, p.25.
140 EOHCS – Belgium 2000, p.25.
141 EOHCS – Belgium 2000, p.25.
142 Anell (1995:22).
143 Saltman (1997:S10).
144 *Facts about the County Councils and Regions 2000*, (2000:3). Within the 20 county councils, are two regions, the Region of Skåne and the Region of Västra Götaland.
145 *Fact Sheets on Sweden* (1999:2).
146 *Facts about the County Councils and Regions 2000*, (2000:6).
147 Sjöberg (2001:5).
148 *Facts about the County Councils and Regions 2000*, (2000,11).
149 EOHCS – Sweden 2001, p.25.
150 Saltman and von Otter (1992:38).
151 Saltman and von Otter (1992:39).

152 Saltman (1997:S10).
153 Sjöberg (2001:3).
154 The Ministry of Health and Social Affairs also has a supervisory role over the country councils. The Ministry may legislate temporary ceilings on county councils and municipal tax rates. For more details see EOHCS – Sweden 2001, p.11.
155 EOHCS – Sweden 2001, p.37.
156 The Swedish Institute (1999:2).
157 The Swedish Institute (1999:2).
158 *Facts about the County Councils 2000* (2000:11).
159 EOHCS – Sweden 2001, p. 28.
160 EOHCS – Sweden 2001, p. 29. It should be no noted that the ceiling for individual co-payments for prescribed drugs is separated from other healthcare services. For prescribed drugs the patient must pay the full cost up to SEK 900, after which the share of patient co-payment is reduced. There is also a ceiling of SEK 1800 for outpatient prescribed drugs over a 12 month period.
161 van Kemenade (1993:78).
162 Source: OECD Health Data 2000.
163 Petersson (1991).
164 EOCHS – Sweden 2001, p. 30.
165 EOCHS – Sweden 2001, p.30.
166 EOCHS – Sweden 2001, p. 30.
167 The Swedish Institute (1999:3).
168 The Swedish Institute (1999:3).
169 The Swedish Institute (1999:3).
170 EOCHS – Sweden 2001, p.40.
171 EOCHS – Sweden 2001, p.21.
172 EOCHS – Sweden 2001, p. 40.
173 EOCHS – Sweden 2001, p.53.
174 The following draws heavily from Harrison and Calltorp (2000).
175 Harrison and Calltorp (2000:237).
176 Harrison and Calltorp (2000:237).
177 Harrison and Calltorp (2000:225)
178 Diderichsen (1999:2)
179 EOCHS – Sweden 2001, p. 87.
180 EOCHS – Sweden 2001, p.88.
181 Stockholm County Council web site (www.sll.se), 9/7/01.
182 News Release, Capio AB, Göteborg Sweden, December 15, 2000.
183 Barbro Naroskyin "Background information for discussion on Capio" Stockholm County County, September 5, 2001, p.1.

184 Barbro Naroskyin (2001:1).
185 Whitehead, Margaret, Rolf Å Gustafsson and Finn Diderichsen (1997:936).
186 Harrison and Calltorp (2000:236).
187 Davoren (2001:1).
188 Davoren (2001:2).
189 Doyle and Bull (2000:564).
190 Price and Pollock (2002:293-294) point out that in 1994, the United Kingdom failed to protect its policy making powers or right to regulate commercial hospital services, unlike Belgium and France. They argue that this failure could have "profound effects on the hospital system, creating uncertainty about the determination of key policy areas such as licensing and qualifications requirements, service volume and quality, and the necessity of public policy."
191 Economist.com (2003).
192 Birchard (2003).
193 Thorpe (2003).
194 The Economist (2003).
195 Aris (2003).
196 Aris (2003).
197 Altenstetter (2003:41-42).
198 Rodwin (2003:35).
199 Rodwin (2003:36).
200 Schokkaert and Van de Voorde (2003:17).
201 It is possible that higher *quality* in terms of a medical procedure could mean higher marginal costs or higher average costs. If higher quality medical procedures require higher levels of fixed costs, this would suggest higher average costs.
202 See Tirole (1998: 212-213).
203 Wagstaff (1991:22). For a further discussion of this issue, see Culyer (1989).
204 For example, in emergency rooms the relative condition of individuals may or may not be known by the other individuals in the waiting room.
205 A parallel might be instructive. Consider an individual who takes a vehicle to a garage for automobile servicing only to be told that he/she would have to wait until more important and significant repairs were made to other vehicles. This method is in contrast to an allocation method based on first come first served.
206 The most common definition of efficiency used in economics is that the allocation of resources should maximize the unweighted sum of consumer and producer surplus.

207 See Boadway (1997).
208 With tradeable claims to health services, the resulting allocation of medical services would approach the allocation by willingness to pay, the difference attributable to the efficiency of the resulting trading system.
209 Martin and Smith (1999:143).
210 See Cullis, Jones and Propper (2000) for a good introduction to the literature on waiting lists as applied to healthcare. Recent work includes Propper (1995), Iversen (1997), Bishai and Lang (2000), Propper et al. (2002), Gravelle, Dusheiko and Sutton (2002), Olivella (2002), Hoel and Saether (2003), Farnworth (2003).
211 Hoel and Saether (2003:600) discuss this issue. Also see Worthington (1987) for a fuller discussion of the issue of the relationship between hospital waiting lists and capacity levels.
212 For a good introduction to peak load pricing see Boadway and Wildasin (1984:180-185), in particular the discussion regarding the rules governing the optimal choice of capacity. Whether peak load pricing is feasible in the healthcare system requires further sudy.
213 Martin and Smith (1999:143).
214 Cullis and Jones (1986:250).
215 Cullis and Jones (1986:250).
216 Locock (2000:92).
217 The State of Oregon 11 member health services commission, comprised of professional and lay people drew up a list of around 700 pairs of conditions and treatments that were to be given priority for funding. According to Ham (1998:7) the most important lesson to be learnt from Oregon's experience is that explicit priority setting tends to result in an increase over time in the basic healthcare package.
218 Locock (2000:91).
219 King and Maynard (1999:52).
220 King and Maynard (1999:52).
221 It is important to note that in Canada, a number of provinces charge a lump sum healthcare premium.
222 Folland et al (2001:611-612) define a deductible as "the amount of healthcare charges for which a beneficiary is responsible before the insurer begins payment" while coinsurance (rate) is defined as "the share of costs that are paid by the beneficiary of a health policy (often after some deductible)". See Folland, Goodman and Stano (1997), Chapter 11, for an introduction to a number of issues related to health insurance.
223 For a formal analysis of this problem see Rothschild and Stiglitz (1976).
224 Tobin (1996:288).
225 Tobin (1996:288).

226 Year Book Australia 2003. Health: Private Health Insurance, Australian Bureau of Statistics.
227 Hopkins and Frech III (2001:226).
228 As described by Hopkins and Frech III (2001:228) the regulatory change allowed anyone who was insured by the age of 30 (or older person prior the cut-off date of June 30, 2000) to take advantage of a base premium. For those joining after the deadline, the base premium increases by 2 percent for each year the individual is over 30 with a ceiling of 70 percent over the base premium. For example, someone aged 43 joining after the deadline would pay a rate of 26 percent over the base premium.
229 Hopkins and Frech III (236-237).
230 The insurer might expect the homeowner to take reasonable precautions to prevent a fire, but may find that fire alarms and other safety devices are not working.
231 See also David Gratzer *Code Blue: Reviving Canada's Healthcare System*, ECW Press, 1999, for a discussion of Medical Savings Accounts.
232 Pauly and Goodman (1995:128).
233 Pauly and Goodman (1995:129-133).
234 Woolhandler, Campbell, and Himmelstein (2003:768).
235 Woolhandler, Campbell, and Himmelstein (2003:773).
236 Aaron (2003:802).
237 Specifically, to minimize the overall cost of providing healthcare, inputs should be chosen such that the ratio of their marginal productivities equals the ratio of the input prices.
238 Hospitals are somewhat like airports which provide services which are complements to airlines. To make the parallel closer, the physicians play a similar role as the airline owners.
239 If the demand is such that two firms can produce at minimum efficient scale then the optimal market structure is production by 2 firms. However, in some cases demand is such that only one firm can produce at minimum efficient scale. The optimal market structure is a natural monopoly, or single firm production.
240 Dranove (1998:71).
241 Folland et. al (1997:307).
242 Folland et. al (1997:308). Folland et al. discuss a number of additional studies in which the results are less robust regarding economies of scope.
243 See Williamson (1976) for a discussion of the feasibility of implementing franchise bidding.

244 Fully distributed cost pricing attempts to allocate a share of the fixed costs on the basis of some observable measure. For example, regarding the cost of surgeries, if 50% of the surgeries are hip replacements then, using fully distributed cost pricing 50% of the common costs should be allocated to hip replacement services. Ramsey pricing is a method of raising prices for different services to meet a total fixed cost constraint in order to minimize allocative inefficiency. For a fuller discussion of these points see Viscusi, Vernon and Harrington Jr. (2000).
245 Grytten and Sørenson (2001:392).
246 Grytten and Sørenson (2001:392).
247 Folland et al. (1997:181).
248 Usually the concern is that a country spends too little on education.
249 This is part of the reason for the popularity of HMO's (Health Management Organizations) in the United States.
250 Bishai and Lang (2000:228) argue that from these estimates one would have to take into account the deadweight costs of additional public revenue generation. In addition, if more private provision is permitted to reduce the queue, any costs in the form of negative externalities borne by citizens through the loss in the value they place on the equity of universal social financing would have to be subtracted as well.
251 Tobin (1996:288).
252 Doyal and Doyal (1999:374).
253 They acknowledge there is a possibility that the overall demand for elective surgeries may increase with the introduction of a private sector, but the increased demand would not be large enough to change their conclusion.
254 See Blomqvist and Carter (1997) for a discussion of this point. They argue that their empirical results cast doubt on the notion of healthcare being a luxury.
255 Baumol (1993).
256 Baumol (1993: 17). For a critique of the sources of slower productivity growth, see Ferris and West (1996), who argue that the slower productivity growth in these areas can be traced to their structural organization, which include public monopolies and large bureaucracies.
257 This is not to say that all funds collected for a program are used within the program. For example, the surplus in the EI account in Canada has been the subject of much political discussion.

258 In Manitoba, it has been suggested that young males pay less, while older drivers pay more, for automobile insurance under the public system than they would under a purely private system. In Manitoba, individuals seen as higher risks, through the accumulation of driving infractions, pay more for their driver's licence and also pay a somewhat higher premium for their auto insurance. premium.
259 In Manitoba, the Manitoba Public Insurance Corporation owns a number of claim centers, which is a combination of a garage and administrative office.
260 In many Canadian provinces, support for private education is provided by grants from provincial governments which come out of general revenues. In this way, the use of a "education voucher" is avoided.
261 Propper (2000:856). In an empirical study using, British Household Panel Survey data (BHPS), Propper shows that the use of private care is strongly related to income, and a set of identifiable individual demographic characteristics and political attitudes. Propper shows that there is an identifiable private welfare class but also shows that there is considerable movement of individuals over time between the public and private sectors. In particular, private use in the past is significantly associated with current use, for both NHS and private care.
262 The issue of the control over the supply of healthcare personnel is central to any proposed expansion in the role of the private sector, if that increases the total amount of healthcare services provided.
263 Laffont and Tirole (2000:219).
264 Gabel et al.(1989) and Jensen et al. (1997).
265 Cutler et al. (1998:1).
266 A notable difference, at least in the Canadian case, is that the only bargaining that occurs is between the Province and the respective monopoly healthcare organization, for example, physicians or nurses.
267 Cutler et al. (1998:41).
268 Robinson (2001:155).
269 Robinson (2001:149).
270 Robinson (2001:157).
271 Robinson (2001:173).
272 Globerman and Vining (1998:57).
273 Propper (2000:856). See also Gray (1998: 911-912) for a similar view.
274 Saltman and Von Otter (1992:91-92).
275 Globerman and Vining (1998:66).

276 Globerman and Vining (1998:67). Their empirical study based on a set of OECD countries does not support the claim that private financing of healthcare contributes to reduced access to publicly financed healthcare. Rather, their results support the view that restricting the availability of private healthcare financing erodes support for public plans that are operating with excess demand.

277 This section is drawn from P. Cyrenne "Product Differentiation and the Public Supply of Private Goods" mimeo, 2000. Recently there have been a number of models that have been developed which are relevant to the discussion contained in this section. For example, there is the literature on the public supply of private goods – like healthcare, Epple and Romano (1996), Gouveia (1996), Belsey and Coate (1991) and Ireland (1990). For a model that shares a number of characteristics with the model developed in this section, see Costa and Garcia (2003).

278 For a fuller discussion of this point see P. Cyrenne (2000).

279 Bryan Nicholson (1998) "Private care eases public burden" *Management Today*, p.1-2.

280 Costa and Garcia (2003:596-597).

281 Hurley et al. (2002:2).

282 Hurley et al. (2002:11) cite data which suggests that the number of people who self-insure in Australia is large, between 8-10% of private hospital admissions in the early 1990s were for those who self-insured.

283 Hurley et al. (2002:17-18).

284 Currie, Donaldson and Lu (2003:227).

285 Currie, Donaldson and Lu (2003:230).

286 Currie, Donaldson and Lu (2003:233).